DR. LEE SALK

What Every Child Would Like Parents to Know About Divorce

D0388953

HARPER & ROW, PUBLISHERS
NEW YORK, HAGERSTOWN, SAN FRANCISCO, LONDON

FIRST EDITION

Designed by Gloria Adelson

Library of Congress Cataloging in Publication Data

Salk, Lee, date
   What every child would like parents to know about
divorce.
   Includes index.
   1. Divorce—United States.   2. Children of divorced
parents.   I. Title.
HQ834.S24   1978   301.42'84   77-3769
ISBN 0-06-013764-9

78 79 80 81 82 83 10 9 8 7 6 5 4 3 2 1

I dedicate this book to all children, everywhere, first among them, my daughter, Pia, and my son, Eric.

CONTENTS

PREFACE

FOR MORE THAN twenty-five years I have worked profession-
ally with people in trouble, both adults and children. Often
divorce was the crisis that brought them to me. I thought
I knew the extent of the anguish that divorce could inflict
on both parents and children. But it was not until I myself
experienced, together with my children, the terrible realities of getting "unmarried" that I fully understood how
deeply this experience reaches into the very heart of one's
existence, testing all of one's strengths and revealing all of
one's weaknesses as a human being. This experience, together with my years as a practicing psychologist, has convinced me that this book was needed and could be useful.

It is intentionally a plain-spoken book. I have no doubt
that some professionals and academically inclined review-

ers will accuse me of being simplistic in my discussion of such profoundly complicated psychological events as separation anxiety, the trauma of grief and loss, self-destructiveness, denial in fantasy, the reality principle, regressive behavior, and other theoretical issues. But I believe it is mistaken to confuse straightforward explanations, simply stated, with oversimplification. Much depends on whom one is addressing and on what occasion.

What I've tried to do here is to provide the essence of what I do in my office for an unhappy parent or a worried child. Following the text of each chapter I have included some of the many questions and problems that have arisen in my professional consultations with patients and my responses to them. It is clear to me that theoretical discussion or statistical documentation is not what is called for at such a time. The parent is in the agony of indecision and guilt, and the child is bewildered and helpless. The questions in their eyes are: What can I do? What *should* I do? What is happening to me? I feel it is my responsibility not to evade their questions and their appeal for help. Theoretical hairsplitting is of no help to them. What I feel I must provide —even when in the kind of doubt that afflicts every responsible clinician—is a discussion of the issues and problems in a way that can be put to practical use. This is what I have attempted to do in this small volume.

CHAPTER 1

HOW DO YOU VIEW
YOUR DIVORCE?

DIVORCE IS UNDOUBTEDLY one of the greatest stresses a human being can experience. It is second only to the distress suffered from the loss of a loved one through death. We must acknowledge that the pain of divorce is understandable and normal. In fact, anyone approaching divorce with calm and composure is probably not facing the situation realistically. There may be moments of relief and even feelings of optimism from time to time as you face your new life ahead, but these will not be your most pervasive or deep-rooted reactions. More often than not, you will also be subject to episodes of emotional and physical weakness, which are entirely appropriate under the circumstances.

When you're told by your friends, "Now, now, you'll get over it, it's probably all for the best," or "Don't take it too

1

much to heart," you'll probably feel even worse. For the most part your divorce involves a complete reversal of the original family goals that existed when you embarked upon your marriage full of eagerness and promise. You anticipated happiness, fulfillment, and companionship, a pleasurable and rewarding commitment to a home and a family. You and your spouse shared a feeling of completeness and interdependence. Your marriage promised you freedom from loneliness and the pleasant anticipation of shared growth. Now the sharing and the glowing promise that marriage held have collapsed. For some this change is abrupt, for others gradual. For some the divorce is felt as a welcome relief, but for many it is an absolute and complete shock.

When divorce strikes, the process of disassembling a family places tremendous demands on the marital partners, and they crave some structure as a guide to dealing with the intense emotional reactions and the uncertainties that divorce causes. Divorce sets up circumstances that are so disorganizing that everyone subjected to it feels overwhelmed and wonders how he or she can make it through. Almost everything in your life that has been stable now must be reorganized. And this uncertainty leaves you in a state of chronic anxiety. The periodic attacks of panic you feel result from the unpredictability of your life, and the intensity of these feelings confirms the fact that this may be one of the most traumatic experiences you have ever encountered.

What is actually happening when divorce becomes imminent? More important, what do you think divorce *means*? Do *you* believe that it is evidence of a major failure in your life which forever after will set limits on your—and your children's—potential for growth and happiness in the future? Your answers to these questions will have a lot to do with determining how you'll deal with the crisis and its aftermath, and much to do with the future of your children. There is ample social evidence to push you into the trap of feeling your divorce will damage you permanently. Rising divorce statistics are constantly cited to reflect a decline in morality in our society. The family environment after divorce is described as a "broken home."

Society has supported the idea that marriage is the culminating opportunity for growth in people's lives. There are no traditional provisions for what happens beyond the breakup of a marriage. Your feelings at the moment confirm this perception that divorce is evidence of a failed life. I believe this line of thought may be quite mistaken and a dangerous oversimplification.

Marriage is a developmental stage in life. For many men and women, so is divorce. Marriages fail for any number of reasons, many of them good reasons for ending a relationship. During the years you and your spouse were married you each went through many changes as a result of intellectual growth, work experiences, and emotional development. At the time you married, there was a greater convergence of feelings and values, goals and ideas about what would make you *both* happy than you and your partner would ever experience again. In looking back to the beginning days of your relationship you will find that you did not bare all your expectations of marriage to your partner. Your spouse probably acted in the same way. In fact, as time passed you found your expectations changing. I have had patients say to me, "But when I got married it was my understanding that we would have our weekends together." The partner responds, "But it was my understanding that we would have a chance to be individuals and do the things that we each like."

All relationships, those that end in divorce as well as

those that don't, undergo these kinds of changes and mis-understandings. In most instances, compromises can be made that do not interfere with the integrity, self-esteem, and goals of the other partner, but in many cases there is little or no room for compromise without stifling the growth and integrity of the other partner.

Every day of your life brings modifications in your thoughts and feelings. Sometimes the partners develop in different directions, or change their expectations, and there is bound to be a marked change in their emotions and often in their feelings toward each other. With all these changes there may come a disenchantment with the mar-riage on the part of one or both spouses. Partners may grow apart rather than together. When this happens re-sentments build, hostility develops, and love is lost. Is it logical or humanly economical to continue life in an un-happy situation that promises little room for happiness in the future, or is it better to modify the situation by agreeing to divorce? When a divorce results from these circum-stances, might it not be more logical to see it as a develop-mental stage of growth rather than a failure? But whether it in fact turns out to be a stage of growth for you will depend upon whether you are able to put the pain of a failed marriage behind you, learn from what has happened, mobilize your resources, and begin the next stage of your life.

In today's world, where people have more options in how to conduct themselves, a wider range of interests and activi-ties, and where change takes place ever more rapidly, insta-bility in marital relationships is bound to occur more fre-quently.

In years past you would have felt compelled to continue living with your spouse regardless of your unhappiness, simply out of commitment to a life together "for better or worse." In those days people maintained fairly traditional, clearly defined roles. Divorce was universally regarded as a failure.

I am not suggesting that marriages be terminated because of "frivolous" fantasies or short-range goals. However, divorce following careful examination of problems, frank self-evaluation, and the insights time provides is another thing entirely. All new creations, new ideas, works of art, scientific developments, involve the rearrangement of factors into patterns that did not previously exist. In fact, scientific development is basically a destructive act arising from frustration. The scientist cannot accept the way things are; he challenges the familiar explanations and observations, and is driven to find a more efficient way of arranging them that renders previously acceptable theories obsolete. In this way progress results from frustration.

So long as two people find contentment built around a happy relationship, they are willing to keep things the way they are. But when this feeling has changed because the relationship is frustrating and no longer conducive to happiness, productiveness, and the satisfactory nurturance of the children, then I see nothing wrong with dissolving the marriage. Some marriages are held together by mutual distrust, anger, and hostility; they offer little pleasure to the partners and the satisfactions are, at best, perverse. We sometimes refer to these as "love-hate" relationships, and although they can persist on this basis, they are essentially destructive.

It is not for me to decide whether it is right or wrong for a particular relationship to come apart, but if it does as a result of a "growth process," there need be no lingering over the remains. One can and should learn from the past, but the important thing is to channel one's energies toward the mobilization of resources so that the next stage in growth can take place. And it will.

A childless marriage that ends in divorce involves only the two people who made the commitment to each other in the first place. When there are children, however, the divorce is qualitatively different. The parents *must always* keep the concerns of their children paramount. This does not mean they should close off their own emotions; of course they will experience regret, pain, liberation—that wide range of feelings inevitable to divorce. But your children didn't cause your marriage, nor are they causing the marriage to come apart.

When a divorce takes place in a marriage that includes children, it should be viewed as an emergency situation that requires dispatch, intelligence, and compassion, in helping to structure an existence for the children that protects their integrity and psychological well-being.

The conventional view is that children should be protected from the ravages of divorce. I agree. But most people interpret this to mean that children should be protected from the divorce process itself, even when decisions are to be made that directly affect their care and well-being. You are often cautioned to hide your feelings from your children, and prevent them from knowing that their home may be disassembled. I believe these views are totally incorrect and often have a destructive rather than a protective effect. In fact, I think they leave your child vulnerable to severe trauma when he or she eventually has to face the reality of what has happened.

Children are very sensitive and aware. They may not be able to articulate what is going on, but believe me, they know something is happening. Concealing arguments and avoiding discussions of marital discord are not convincing to a child. In all likelihood, your marital stress did not begin at any *one* moment but progressed over a period of time.

The tensions, arguments, hostilities between you and your spouse have been a reality in your child's life. Replacing this with silence, indifference, or contrived politeness will do more to raise suspicions in your child's mind than provide him with protection from the fact of your crumbling marriage. In both cases your child is certain to experience emotional distress. It would be ideal if this did not occur, but there is no way of avoiding it. However, these emotional stresses do not necessarily have to lead to permanent consequences for your child. It is possible to prevent lasting damage even if your child has experienced a substantial amount of stress during your turmoil.

Children are far more capable of understanding divorce than many parents realize. In fact, most children, including those whose parents may not be contemplating divorce, wonder about it anyway. The happily married parents of one child I know were confronted with the following question from their four-year-old, who was obviously aware of the realities of marriage and divorce. He returned from nursery school one day and asked his mother, "Mommy, when you and Daddy get divorced, who will I live with?" There was a time when children were likely to have hidden the fact of their parents' divorce, but today the realities of life can be dealt with more openly.

I cannot tell you how many young patients I have seen whose parents had tried to protect them from knowing about their marital discord. Invariably these children suffered from increased anxiety. They reacted subconsciously to their parents' marital problems and had to bear the burden in silence. A child whose parents are open and frank feels far less responsible for family problems than the child whose parents conceal the gravity of the situation. There is no way human beings of any age can be fooled over a long period of time into believing that a tense situation is anything other than a tense situation!

Parents use many different approaches in trying to protect children from marital discord. In years past the most conventional approach was to stay together for the sake of the children. Although many people still hold this view, a recent scientific survey states that two out of three married people do *not* believe parents should stay together for the sake of the children.

I have had many adult patients who told me that when they were children they couldn't wait to leave home because of family tensions or the absence of spontaneous affection between their parents. Over and over again they have said to me, "I wish my parents had divorced and found happiness in another relationship." Other patients whose parents had been divorced admitted that it was difficult for a while, but in the long run, "we were all better off."

A child growing into adulthood in the midst of an unpleasant but intact marriage ends up with a far more negative attitude about marriage than one whose parents were divorced and then entered into another relationship that was substantially more fulfilling. Your child, seeing you work out the problems of your life, as unpleasant as it may be during the process, also gains the experience of realizing that problems can be solved and that people can grow as a result of dealing with them.

Frequently people with unsatisfactory marriages try to sustain them with a minimum of friction, a minimum of interaction, and perhaps little or no love. In one case, a mother and father consulted me about fits of rage, destructiveness, and a sharp drop in school performance in their twelve-year-old son Richard. The parents admitted they lived "lives of their own" and had little to do with each other. They were friendly in passing, but did little or nothing together. Each had friends of his and her own, and occasional affairs with other people. Basically, they wanted to divorce, but were reluctant to take the step. Neither wanted to disrupt the existence of the family and avoided entering into long-term commitments to new partners. They lived from day to day and in the process had become increasingly more alienated from each other and from their children. They met little more than the physical needs of their children. They complained that Richard lacked motivation, seemed bored, and daydreamed a lot. As they described his behavior, they seemed more concerned about the inconvenience or being summoned to school to discuss his behavior than about how upset he was.

After seeing Richard and discussing his feelings with him, I learned a great deal about the roots of his symptoms. No one really cared about him, he said, and his parents rarely talked about "family things." He felt his parents didn't care for each other. When I pointed out to his parents the possibility that he was unhappy about the family situation, they assured me he didn't know anything about it because they had been careful to avoid upsetting him.

Clearly, they were under the illusion that Richard (or any child for that matter) could easily be fooled. Richard was caught in a bind and was very unhappy. His unhappiness was no less intense than that of a child whose parents were in the throes of an acrimonious divorce—and perhaps it was even worse. His mother and father were pursuing clandestine relationships in an attempt at happiness that Richard could never share. He was being protected from everything: parental satisfaction, family warmth, the "trauma of divorce."

Another family chose a different alternative to protect their children from the pain of divorce. To avoid divorce, the father found work in another city to account for the separation. The mother was left with full responsibility for rearing the children, and couldn't cultivate any relationships with men for fear that this would appear to be infidelity, while the father, in effect, abandoned his children. The mother's loneliness and her resentment increased, and her silent anger at her husband was heard as loudly by her children as if she had spoken out against him. The price of sparing them the trauma of divorce was to prevent them from ever seeing either parent as happy or fulfilled. They had no model for a happy relationship, nor were they able to experience the successful resolution of their parents' problems so that the whole family would eventually benefit from a happier existence.

In both families described above, there is no authentic family unity or affection, only a kind of "truce," a not very satisfactory "coexistence." What concerns me about these arrangements is that children who lack a feeling of involvement in a family unit frequently seek out a substitute for family life—a peer group, a gang, or a cult of some sort.

In my view, these children—and many, many others I've seen in my professional practice whose parents chose to avoid divorce to "protect the children"—would have been better off facing the trauma, dealing with it effectively, and achieving a potentially happier outlook on life.

I do not believe parents ever stay together solely for the sake of the children. The reasons for staying together may be deep-rooted and not obvious, but they are invariably reasons built around adult needs, not children's needs. All such arrangements and any sacrifices "for the sake of the children" place a tremendous burden on the children who are supposedly being protected. Under these circumstances adults and children are both denied the possibility of a more gratifying family life.

It is vitally important for children to see parents in a loving relationship. This serves as a model for a child of what a caring relationship is like. Children like seeing their parents happy and joyous, and like to share in their joys and happiness. A family kept together for the sake of the children cannot possibly provide this kind of experience. If the marriage cannot work, the partners must be allowed to become free so that they can find loving relationships elsewhere, which their children can then view as a model.

None of this implies that a divorce can be made pleasant for a child. But divorce *is* a reality for many people, and it can be a far better reality than maintaining a malignant marriage. For a child the damaging aspect of a divorce is not the fact of ending up with divorced parents. The danger lies in the indignities created by some aspects of the legal process, and in the child's possible loss of self-esteem. Legally, children are often treated in the same manner as property. Their feelings and wishes are ignored, they are vulnerable to being used as hostages in a parent's effort to gain material advantages in the settlement, and they may be used as weapons in a vindictive attempt to hurt the other parent.

But when the child's feelings and rights are respected by parents and the legal system, this can serve to demonstrate to the child that the successful resolution of a painful human conflict is possible. The child learns that solutions can be worked out, hard as they are, and that difficulty can lead to positive ends.

If you give your child the opportunity to be heard, you will make an unhappy situation far more endurable. This may sound as if I am saying divorce is good for your child. Certainly not. I am only pointing out that divorce is not *necessarily* bad for your child and need not damage him or her, *if* it is dealt with in a manner that protects the child's integrity. I have seen young people who have come through a divorce who are emotionally much stronger and perhaps more stable for having been through it. They have not been traumatized by the experience, nor are they turned off by marriage itself. Had their parents stayed together "for the sake of the children," in all likelihood they would *not* have come away with a positive attitude about marriage. It is impossible to hide from children the disenchantment unhappy spouses feel with each other.

Now I would like to introduce some of the issues that patients have discussed with me concerning their decision to divorce and my reactions to these issues:

"My wife and I feel that we need a trial separation to decide whether or not we ought to get divorced. I plan to move out for a six-month period so that we can see how things work out and then decide whether we want to come back together again or get divorced. How do we handle this with our daughter?"

The only way to handle it is to be straightforward and honest. Explain to your daughter that neither of you is as happy as you would like to be living together, and that you want to try living apart for a while to see how things work out. Explain that you may decide to continue in this way, and if you do you will get a divorce. On the other hand, each of you may find that by being apart for a while you will be able to sort out your feelings in such a way that it may be possible for you to come back together again and be happier than you are now. Make it clear to her that *she did not cause this to happen.* Affirm your love to your daughter and explain that you are not abandoning her. Tell her that you are going to live elsewhere but will continue to see her and stay in touch.

For the most part, the explanation for a separation is similar to that for a divorce. However, a divorce has more finality to it than does a separation—which is, in a sense, holding the

marriage in suspension. Children generally perceive this difference and at this time may feel a greater internal pressure to
make things work so their parents will come back together
again.

Since children frequently feel in some way or other that they
have caused the marriage to fail, they may feel during a separation that heroic efforts on their part to be obedient or otherwise
change their behavior will miraculously bring their parents
together again. For this reason it is essential for you to emphasize to your children that they have not caused the marital
discord and that the problems need to be solved by the two
of you alone.

"My husband and I continue to share many interests in our
everyday life, but the spark seems to be gone from our marriage. We don't have much of a sex life, and that which we
have means little to me. I do have fantasies about affairs with
other people and I constantly think I would really like to have
a 'wild fling.' I don't think that this is a good reason to get
divorced, but I am afraid it's causing my marriage to erode,
and the weaknesses that I could once tolerate in my husband
now cause me terrible irritation. Is it possible that a dull sex life,
such as mine, could be the cause of my boredom and marital
unhappiness?"

It can certainly play a major role in your dissatisfaction. The
fact that you are consciously aware of the problem and are so
frank with yourself about your desires and fantasies makes me
believe you should do something about resolving this problem.
The interests that you and your husband have continued to
share, in spite of your unhappiness, provide a strong, viable
basis for your marriage. I believe you should discuss the matter
of your sex life with your husband and give serious consideration to approaching a reputable sex clinic or a sex therapist
associated with a medical center. I don't mean to imply that

connection with a medical center is the sole criterion for competency, but there are many clinics and groups that offer such help but lack a responsible professional approach.

No one should be ashamed about having sexual problems such as yours, nor should they feel that it is a sign of weakness to seek help. Fortunately we have reached a point in our social evolution where we can recognize that sexual needs play an important role in one's physical and emotional health.

"After twenty years of marriage, my husband has simply picked up and moved out of the house, after informing me that he can't take my dominating him any longer. My four children, who are now in their middle and late teens, are shocked; my friends and neighbors are shocked; and all of our relatives are shocked. This is the first complaint I have ever heard from him about my being dominating. In fact, I have been very happy with him and he seemed to have been very happy with me. In our community we were viewed as the *ideal* couple. As I see it, I made every effort to make him happy.

"I have searched my soul and looked for every possible clue as to what could have caused him to leave home. He refuses to discuss the matter with me, but simply reiterates that he wants his freedom and doesn't want to be dominated by me any longer. Since he absolutely refuses to discuss this situation openly, I have no alternative but to accept his feelings. My children feel sorry for me and resent their father for what he has done. Their feelings are very reassuring and supportive for me, but I really don't want them to reject their father or to treat me as if they were responsible for my happiness. I don't feel that things are hopeless, but I am certainly discouraged. I want to get my life moving again and am afraid that my feelings of discouragement will prevent it. What can I do?"

It is indeed discouraging for a marriage to come to an end so precipitously. I wonder, and I am sure all your friends, relatives, and you yourself have wondered, what else is bothering your husband. If there is no communication between you, there is no way you can find out, nor any way you can help alleviate his discomfort. I am in no position to determine whether or not you were overly dominating toward you husband, but it would seem that some prior complaint should have been registered so that something could have been done about it.

Being discouraged at the present time is understandable; I am sure you must feel that you will never trust anyone again, no matter how sincere he or she may be. However, you will probably find that through close relationships with your friends, relatives, and children you will feel a resurgence of your trust in people. The toughest part for you, I am sure, is the frustration of not knowing what really caused your husband to terminate the marriage. Twenty years and four children is quite an investment, and understandably you have feelings of helplessness in trying to resolve your dilemma. It's likely that in time his reasons will come to light and you will have some knowledge as to what brought about his unexpected decision to divorce. In the meantime, tell your children honestly that you are perplexed even though their father probably has what he feels are justifiable reasons for divorcing.

Realistically, now you have to build your life around your children, home, and job and not neglect these responsibilities. In this way you will get your life moving again, and the satisfaction this will give you should diminish your discouragement. Ruminating about your husband at this point will not help unless you consult with a professional counselor, who may encourage you to find insights into possible ways you might have played a role in your husband's decision to leave you.

"I want to avoid as much confusion as possible for my three children, and I do not want them to be caught up in my marital difficulties. My husband and I decided to divorce because of our mutual dissatisfaction. We had discussed the matter, made the decision to divorce, and explained it to our children. They were not happy with the idea, but seemed to accept it reasonably well. It's been four weeks since we discussed our divorce with them, and we have now decided we would like to reconcile our differences and make one last try to keep our marriage together. I'm afraid this will be very confusing to our children, although it's exactly what they wanted us to do. If our reconciliation doesn't work and we eventually decide to divorce, I'm afraid our children will suffer doubly. Do you think it's a sign of weakness on our part to change our minds in this way? And are we making a mistake?"

Absolutely not. I believe people should explore every opportunity to make their marriage work as long as they feel there is any hope. It's important to feel you've tried every possible avenue and "walked that last mile." Don't hesitate at a reconciliation, even including compromises that you might not have previously thought you would make.

Some outsiders might view your compromises as being unrealistic, but it's always easier for someone who is not involved in your marriage to offer this kind of advice. Frequently, married people on the brink of divorce are told by others, "A clean break is better for everyone involved. If you hesitate it means down deep you are clinging to a bad situation—perhaps you are masochistic and that is why you want it to continue." Whether or not they are right in the long run, you owe it to yourself to try again.

When marital trouble first arises, a divorce seems like the best, easiest, and wisest way out. That is because at this time divorce is simply an *idea,* and not a reality. As it becomes a reality and you get down to the grueling details of divorce, it's natural that you'll ask yourself, "Is it worth trying again?" Again, don't hesitate to get help from the most competent professional counselor you can find.

If after trying that last time, you still decide to divorce, the disappointment to your children will be renewed but it will not necessarily be more intense. In fact, you will have shown them the seriousness of your desire to save the marriage and will have provided them with a model for working out the kinds of complex problems life sometimes presents.

"My wife and I have had our ups and downs in marriage. Lately we have been having more downs than ups and I think we are going to have to prepare for divorce. We can't afford expensive lawyers and don't know where to turn for help. We are not poverty-stricken, but at the same time we would be financially wiped out if we were to retain separate lawyers, even if their fees were modest. Where can we turn in such a situation?"

Most communities have family service agencies that are staffed by social workers and other professionals who are trained to help people with family problems. They are available to offer counseling on family matters and are knowledgeable about other resources in your community that provide legal assistance. In addition to family service agencies, there are community mental health clinics and consultation services. Many clergy of various denominations are active in counseling and assisting families in crisis.

Although the ability to hire independent professionals gives you greater freedom of choice in getting the kind of help you need, you are by no means left out in the cold because you are financially limited. A little searching should turn up a matrimonial lawyer whose fees are low enough for you to afford. Even a lawyer you can't afford could recommend someone whose fees are within your reach. Don't hesitate to call more than one and gather as many suggestions as you can to help you decide how to proceed.

"My wife wants a divorce. She claims she has no chance to develop her own interests, because the marriage prevents her from doing so. She wants all the household belongings, the children, and everything I've got and ever will have! I'm absolutely stunned by this, because we have spent all of our married years building a future for our family. I want the marriage to continue and feel she is simply going through a phase. I wish I could do something about it, but I can't. I frankly feel that her best friend, who is having marital trouble, is inciting her. It's impossible for me to talk to her at this point since she's beyond reason.

"Now I'm so angry and frustrated I'd like to make her life as miserable as possible and will do anything to prevent her from getting *anything* from me. At this point I couldn't care less about *her,* wouldn't have her back if I could, and yet something tells me she'll regret the move she's making. I truly believe in this instance it's best to fight fire with fire, but perhaps in anger I am making the wrong decision."

Your immediate reaction of intense anger is clearly understandable. However, bear in mind that you yourself feel she may be going through a phase. Moreover, your basic wish is to remain together. If you take a strong, angry stance and try to annihilate her psychologically, you may provide her with enough justification for leaving and make it impossible for her to change her mind about the divorce. You need not give in to her demands, but at the same time you should not incite her to the point of no return; you will simply be venting your anger and accomplishing nothing. If you can keep yourself relatively calm she might indeed come out of what you consider to be a phase and want to return to the marriage. If she doesn't, and wants to pursue the divorce, your composure might help her to be more rational in discussing matters with you.

Being rational and maintaining a cool attitude, even in the midst of the turmoil of divorce, helps to maintain your self-respect and minimizes the chances of your children getting caught up in the anger between the two of you. This approach does not mean you are weak, nor that you will allow yourself to be taken advantage of. It does, however, set the stage for a possible reconciliation if your wife has a change of heart.

"My wife and I are among the few couples in our community who are still married. The majority of our neighbors and friends have either been divorced, are getting divorced, or are having sufficient marital difficulties to consider divorce. What does all this mean! Where are we going? Is the institution of marriage finished, and are we old-fashioned in maintaining it?"

I believe that marriage as an institution is here to stay. I believe that children can best develop emotionally in a home where there are two loving and involved parents. I further believe that while all relationships undergo some stress, most people are happiest when they have a stable relationship where there is mutual respect and each partner recognizes the individuality and integrity of the other. I believe the divorce rate, which has been rising rapidly, will reverse itself in the not too distant future. Clearly the family as an institution has undergone a great deal of change. There are fewer forces within our present society that support the integrity of the family as a unit; in fact, most pressures are directed at pulling the family apart. Many people have given up traditional family roles. Women have increasingly chosen activities away from the home, and many men have found themselves shaken by the disappearance of traditional home life. The sexual revolution has enticed many people away from the idea that love, sex, and marriage are intricately bound together.

I believe that many of the people you know who are divorced, or divorcing, are unhappy because of divergent goals, expectations, and opportunities they have developed since they were married. In the future I believe people will get married for different reasons, and will have goals and expectations that are consistent with the social and cultural changes brought about by such forces as the sexual revolution and the women's movement. Perhaps fewer people will get married and those who marry will have fewer children. The reasons for marriage will, however, be more consistent with the changed values and life styles, which in turn will result in fewer divorces.

CHAPTER 2

WHAT TO TELL YOUR CHILD

How AND WHAT you tell your child about your decision to divorce depends to a great extent upon the circumstances, particularly the immediate ones, that precipitated the divorce. How and what you tell your child also depends upon the child's age, although I believe the same approach should be taken regardless of the child's age so long as he or she can engage in some kind of discussion. If your child is too young to comprehend, obviously there is no explanation you can offer—until later on.

I am sure many parents reading this book would like to have me present word for word what to say to their child. Needless to say, this is impossible. My suggested explanations and approaches are simply guidelines for handling the problem; the age of your child, her capacity for comprehension, and her level of emotional maturity should be determining factors in how you apply my recommendations. The information I offer is meant to help you understand the needs of your child and to see the problems that divorce creates *from your child's point of view*.

I believe it is best to be straightforward with your child in explaining your divorce. Use direct terms and avoid ambiguity as much as possible. Be specific; avoid abstractions. If you remember that divorce can be a developmental stage for you and your spouse, your explanation will flow more easily, and be more easily understood and accepted by your child.

I suggest you tell your child—in your own words, of course—that "when we first met and got to know each other well we began to love one another very, very much. We decided we wanted to live together and do things together. We were happy with each other and decided we wanted to have children. As time went on, some things began to change and did not work out the way we thought they would, or the way we wanted them to. Now we find that the love we had before is no longer there and that we are not happy living together any longer. We have tried to work things out, but there does not seem any way we can. Because of this we have decided that it is best to stop being unhappy together and to live more happily apart from each other. That is why we have decided to get unmarried, which is what we call a divorce."

It should be evident that this explanation covers only part of what is on your child's mind. It attempts to explain *your* needs and addresses itself to *your* past unhappiness and *your* hope for a better life. But what of your child? No matter how miserable home life has been, there are children who would prefer keeping the family and home intact. Therefore, you *must* speak to the questions which now—or soon will—crowd your child's mind about his or her prospects for future happiness.

It is essential that you stress right from the beginning that "even though your mother (or father) and I are not happy with *each other* and no longer love one another, we still love *you*. You will always be our child no matter what else happens, and just because we don't love each other does not mean that you can't continue to love both of us." Make sure you get this crucial point across; how your child deals with his own feelings about the divorce and about each of the parents depends upon it.

A child's loyalty to both parents is deep-rooted and undergoes a great deal of stress when she learns that her parents are no longer committed to one another. For this reason, she is bound to question whether or not your love for her will be jeopardized if she continues to show love for the spouse *you* no longer love, and toward whom you may feel angry and vindictive.

These, then, should be the basic themes of your explanation, but the words and the degree of detail need to be tailored to your child's age, level of understanding, and emotional maturity. You know your child best and should be able to choose the right words to get the basic points across. Teenagers may have more detailed questions following your explanation, but they may also remain silent. On the other hand, a curious four-year-old may stun you with specific questions that go right to the heart of the matter.

The approach I have recommended may not cover all the main elements of your own divorce, but I am sure it will serve to some degree in all cases. Keep in mind that you need not present all the details in your initial explanation. In fact, it is wise not to. For this reason, the wording in my suggested explanation should be useful regardless of the combination of elements that apply in your case.

The facts of your decision to divorce, and your child's worries about the future, should always be the focus of your initial explanation. You should *not* burden the child with a litany of wrongs you have suffered; you must control any acrimonious feelings you may have toward your spouse. Focus on your child's needs and questions rather than allow this moment to become an occasion when you release *your* feelings. Avoid placing the child in the impossible position of having to absorb the upsetting news of the divorce and also take sides in what is happening between his parents. This is especially true if your spouse has initiated the divorce or is leaving you for someone else. It's hard to do, but I assure you it is in your child's best interest.

You can be certain that your child will eventually ask many questions that will allow you to deal with his concerns, and yours, more fully. But, to repeat, do not overload your child with too much difficult-to-assimilate information too quickly.

When should you tell your child? I believe the best time is as soon as the decision is made, with a few exceptions. For example, if your child is away at summer camp it might be best to wait for her to return, rather than to rush off and give an explanation at a time when there's little or no opportunity to ask follow-up questions.

It has been my experience that in dealing with more than one child, it does not matter whether they are told separately or together. You are in a better position to make this decision than anyone else. However, if your children are close in age and can understand things at a similar level, it may be best to speak to them together. In this way you will avoid the problems that sometimes occur if you forget to tell one child something you told the other. Since it is such a delicate matter to begin with, this could cause a child to feel you are holding something back from him. It is important to create an atmosphere in which your children will feel free to raise questions, express their feelings, and get as much out in the open as possible—when they feel ready to do so. You should plan to tell your children in as comfortable a setting as you can arrange. You know where they feel relaxed and comfortable, and where there will be privacy.

You can be sure that each of your children will want to talk to each parent separately. This should be encouraged and, again, every effort should be made to answer the child's questions directly without assaulting your spouse's integrity and character. Remember that whatever you may think of your spouse at this moment, he or she will continue to be your child's parent, and your child's feelings toward both of you and himself will be markedly influenced by what you say. You can also be sure that your children will be speaking with each other about the divorce when they are alone. Their uncertainties and emotional reactions will tend to reinforce one another and perhaps arouse more anxiety than existed before. For this reason you should encourage them to come back to you from time to time to discuss any other questions that might arise.

In some cases a divorce or separation occurs because one parent simply picks up and leaves the family with little or no explanation. Since abandonment is often a child's worst fear, this unexpected event is particularly upsetting. "Why did Daddy go away?" "Why did Mommy leave us?" Perhaps the best explanation to offer is a general one that applies to most, if not all, situations where abandonment has taken place. "Daddy (or Mommy) believed that he simply couldn't find happiness in our family and had to go someplace else to make a different life." You might add, "I know you miss him and wonder how he is, where he's living, and what he's doing. I wonder too, and maybe he will write or call us and we can find out. Even though you miss him, you're probably angry too that he did this without letting us know. It's selfish and not very nice, but I guess he felt he couldn't explain it to us."

In some situations there are specific reasons for a parent's leaving, and these can be offered as part of the explanation. *Make it clear, however, that your child did not cause this to happen.* Most children fear that they have done something wrong which caused the other parent to go away. Did their misbehavior, trouble at school, or some other problem cause the parent such anguish that he left home? No child should live with such a burden, and the remaining parent must offer constant reassurance to alleviate any guilt.

Some children have expressed their feelings to me about an abandoning parent and wondered if perhaps they didn't show enough love to that parent, which in turn caused the abandonment. In all cases emphasize to the child that he or she had *nothing* to do with causing the abandonment. This point must be reiterated from time to time during any discussions which come up.

Ideally it is best if both parents together tell the children of their decision to divorce. I am assuming, of course, that you and your spouse are civil to each other and can conduct a calm discussion. If, as is frequently the case, your feelings of bitterness are so intense that you tend to attack one another rather than the issue, then it's better if each parent explains the divorce separately to the children.

No matter how angry or vindictive you feel, avoid making derogatory remarks about your spouse to your child and make every effort to protect his or her integrity. I am not suggesting you be dishonest or "whitewash" your spouse. Your child would only become more confused and find it difficult to deal effectively with his own feelings. I have known some parents who have even referred to their spouses in glowing terms in an effort to ease the child's apprehensions. This simply does not work. It serves to weaken your own credibility. One child, with the kind of precise logic children are more often capable of than we realize, asked me, "Why does he want to divorce her, if she is such a *wonderful,* wonderful person?"

In the course of interpreting your divorce to your child, tell her, "I know this is upsetting to you, and I know you don't want it to happen." Explain that you understand she must be wondering about many things having to do with the divorce. Let her know you will try to answer all her questions and help her deal with these unhappy feelings. You may find it helpful, as I did with my own children, to emphasize that if you could, you would stay together, but that you have come to feel it would be best for everyone involved, including your child, if you and your spouse lived apart. Be sure to explain why this is so. Say something like, "When I'm happy, it's easier for me to make you happy. When I'm unhappy, it's hard for me to be the kind of parent you need and enjoy." Tell her that even though you will be living apart, you will each be doing things with her and you are each still her parent and will love her as much as always.

Some parents are afraid to explore a child's feelings about divorce. Children sense this fear and become reluctant to talk. You need to convey a sense of trust, as well as a sense of strength, in dealing with your child's apprehensions. If you are half-hearted in your desire to explore his feelings, you will not succeed at it. You must recognize the importance of allowing his feelings to come out and feel confident that you can cope with them. While I am emphasizing the importance of getting a child to talk about his feelings, I am not suggesting you pressure him into talking. There is no way you can pull feelings out of a child. Getting him to express himself is a subtle process that involves patience on your part. In a sense you must give him permission to talk, while you watch his reactions, listen to what he says, and pay attention to what he *doesn't* talk about.

People are funny in the way they try to reassure you about your unpleasant feelings. They think they are being compassionate when they say "You *shouldn't* feel so unhappy," or "You *shouldn't* feel so anxious," or "You *shouldn't* feel so lonely." Telling someone he *shouldn't* feel a certain way never works. Those who give this kind of advice don't know it, but they are threatened by your feelings. They can't handle your feelings of unhappiness, anxiety, or loneliness, so they tell you that you shouldn't feel that way. There's little reassurance in their remarks. In fact, it frequently makes you feel worse! A person with compassion acknowledges your feelings, accepts them, and wants to help you overcome them.

Even if your child is eager to talk about his feelings, he may need a good deal of encouragement from you; and, of course, if he's reluctant to express himself, he is going to need even more encouragement from you. The manner of your approach, even the wording you use, can play an important role in giving a child permission to let loose.

As a psychologist who has spent considerable time interviewing children about some of their innermost feelings, I have found it helpful to let a child know I understand his difficulty in expressing himself. I have used openings like "I know it is tough to talk about some things—and this must be one of them—but I am sure you have feelings about it, maybe lots of mixed-up feelings, and sometimes you get to feel better when you talk about them." Such assertions frequently cause a child to verbalize his feelings quite spontaneously.

This method works for teenagers as well as young children. Essentially, my approach to children is no different from that to adults. The words may vary, but the import is the same. I don't believe in talking down to children, and they don't appreciate it either.

You should be aware of the questions and doubts that flood your child's mind at this time, whether he voices them or not:

"Who will take care of me?"

"Will I be left alone?"

"Where will I live?"

"Will I still be able to be with both of you?"

"What will happen if I get sick?"

"Will we live in the same house?"

"Who will feed me?"

"Will you still be my Mommy and Daddy?"

"Will I be with my brothers and sisters?"

The first fear of all children is that of abandonment. Children fear losing the adults who are closest to them and on whom they depend for the greatest amount of love and emotional support. They are deeply worried about being separated from those places, objects, and people that have been part of their everyday life. This fear may cause them to cling to some of those things, which are in a sense a remembrance of the emotional security they felt during the time the marriage was intact.

"Does anyone else know about the divorce?" "What should I tell my friends?" These questions are not likely to be of immediate concern to your child right after you have informed him of the impending divorce, but offering help in telling others is important at this time, in advance of the problem. Tell your child who knows and who does not know. If for some reason you plan to keep it private for any length of time, let him know this. If it is not a private matter, tell him you intend to let friends and relatives know and that he too can feel free to tell his friends.

Some children find it a burden to tell others about a divorce, others appear indifferent to the matter, and still others seem eager to get it out in the open. Explain to your child that some people may sound shocked and react as if this were a terrible tragedy. Others may become very curious and want to know all the details of what is going on and what caused it. Suggest that she explain it to others in much the same way you have explained it to her. If she prefers to avoid the subject altogether with friends and relatives, support her in that wish. Let her know, however, that people will eventually get to know about it and may come to her with questions. It is understandable if your child takes the attitude that she does not want to discuss the matter even if people ask questions. Tell her the best way to handle it is by simply saying, "I would rather not talk about it."

In all likelihood your child has friends whose parents are divorced, and has heard about the problems and pleasures in his friends' lives. This is an important point for you to raise immediately with your child in discussing the divorce, because of his preconceptions. Ask him how these friends feel about their lives with their divorced parent. Some children may be scarred by the bitter struggles that can precede a divorce. On the other hand, you may be surprised to find that many children brag about the fact that they have not one but two families, and admit to having more fun now that their parents are divorced than they did before. Some children enjoy having two rooms, in two different homes, with two sets of toys, games, and clothes. While this situation hardly measures up to the "recommended standard" for family life, children may not see divorce as a traumatic event and may even find it a welcome improvement in their circumstances.

If your child seems reluctant to discuss the divorce with

you, you might suggest: "Perhaps you'll feel more comfortable talking to another person, like a doctor who works with children, and who will keep whatever you say private and confidential." It is sometimes far easier for a child to discuss her feelings with someone who is not emotionally involved in the situation. This applies equally to any period surrounding the divorce—before, during, or after. Some children find it very difficult to discuss their feelings with a parent, simply because of the highly emotional circumstances surrounding the divorce. And the difficulty is compounded if the child has witnessed many arguments and fights between the parents.

You must recognize the limits of your capabilities in getting your child to express her feelings. I do not mean to imply that you should give up easily, but do recognize that she may not be able to unburden herself to you. Try to provide a conducive atmosphere and then be patient in offering encouragement. *Do not pry.*

Do not be afraid to admit that you do not know the answers to some of your child's questions. If you don't know where he will live or how often he will see each of his parents, say, "We haven't worked out the answers to these questions yet, but we will try to do it in the best possible way for you. I am sure you are not happy about the divorce, but we will try to make things work out as best we can according to the way you would like them to be."

If you fabricate an answer simply to alleviate the uncertainty, you may be giving misinformation which could ultimately shake your child's trust in you. Honesty is essential; you will only undermine the child's sense of security if you lie or make promises you may not be able to keep.

For example, one mother who consulted me had promised her children that when the divorce was over she would get great sums of money and be able to buy them many things. She spoke with absolute certainty in spite of the fact that the divorce was heading to court for adjudication. Her efforts to brighten the picture for her children are understandable, but nevertheless questionable. As it turned out, she did not get the settlement she sought; she was unable to deliver what she promised, which left her children doubtful of any other promises she made in the future.

In my experience working with children, I have learned that they have a tremendous capacity for adjusting to difficult situations. The more they understand, and the more you prepare them for what will take place, the better they are able to handle the stress of a new situation. If they are forewarned that something will cause unhappiness, they are prepared for it and mobilize resources to cope with the problem. If you respect children's feelings, deal with them honestly, and treat them with dignity, you can be sure that a stressful situation or crisis can serve to strengthen their resources during the difficult period. Do not try to suppress your child's reaction or belittle his feelings. Show your understanding and support.

A wide variety of problems have been presented to me by patients when telling their children about their divorce. The examples related below highlight some of the many issues brought up.

"I can't believe my fourteen-month-old child knows we are getting divorced, yet he has been very fidgety lately and wakes up crying. It's hard for me to leave him with a sitter, and he clings desperately to my husband and me even though we haven't had arguments in front of him. It seems as if he senses that something is wrong, and we don't know how to handle him since he is too young to understand any explanations. What could possibly be on his mind?"

Babies this age, and even younger, are extremely sensitive to what is going on around them. While they cannot understand the specific problem, they will show fretfulness and irritability in response to your own anxieties. Studies have repeatedly shown that disturbances in mother/infant interaction, even in the early weeks and months of life, can cause growth problems, digestive disorders, and other dysfunctions. When parents are happy and content they tend to hold their infants in a relaxed and tender way. A parent may express stress through gruff or abrupt movements. Babies are also sensitive to your tone of voice and facial expression.

Many parents have come to me for help because their baby had become unbearably irritable under stressful circumstances. In my experience this build-up of intense irritability occurs because of a circular problem: the parents are under stress and their tolerance for frustration is considerably lowered; their frustration is sensed by the baby, who becomes fretful, which in turn places greater stress on the parents, which increases the baby's irritability.

Obviously if you can diminish the amount of stress you are under, relax more, and show greater tenderness and warmth to your child, the problem will diminish. However, this is more easily said than done when you are faced with the disruption of a divorce. Whatever you can do toward that goal would show up in a more positive reaction from your child.

Your baby obviously gains solace from being held by his parents, and senses some disruption in that satisfaction. If each of you makes a special effort to offer comfort to your baby, particularly when he is tired and about to go to sleep, you will probably be able to break the cycle that is causing you so much anguish. Try to relax your muscles and concentrate on reducing tension during those times. Your relaxation will be felt by your baby, and will serve to make him feel more secure.

"My husband and I are about to get divorced and we have explained this to our five-year-old son, who is our only child. We spoke to him together and explained our getting divorced in a very calm manner. We thought he would cry and be upset, but instead he got very angry with both of us and said he hated us and didn't want us as his mother and father anymore. We are confused by his reaction, but even more confused by the fact that in between his fits of rage he wants to be cuddled, and insists I stay close to him at night as he goes off to sleep. Isn't this unusual?"

No, it is not unusual. He is both angry and frightened. He resents you and needs you at the same time. He needs to release his anger, but at the same time wants the comfort of your presence, particularly when he has to face the transition from the waking world to the unknown world of sleep. Under normal circumstances children have some difficulty going to sleep without the presence of a parent or the security of a familiar object.

When your son told you that he no longer wanted you as a mother and father, it was in a sense like telling you that he was going to divorce you before you divorced each other. It was an attempt on his part to gain mastery over the situation rather than be victimized by it. Show your acceptance of his feelings by explaining that you understand why he is upset and angry, but that no matter how angry he feels now you will still be his parents and will continue to love him. It is important for him to feel free to express these apparently divergent feelings, but at the same time to feel that you love him and accept him regardless of how angry he feels.

It is always hard for parents to tell children about an impending divorce, and it certainly doesn't make it easier when you are faced with an enraged child torn by a conflicting emotions.

"My son Harry keeps asking me why I try to get him to tell me his feelings. I want to know his feelings so we can work things out for his greatest happiness. He seems a little suspicious. What does all this mean?"

Even under the best of circumstances a child may be reluctant to talk to a parent. Do not pressure your son; in all likelihood when he feels comfortable he will discuss his concerns with you. In the course of encouraging Harry to discuss his feelings, it is essential that you let him know that his feelings are going to be a very important consideration in working out future arrangements. Let him know that his needs and wishes will not be ignored and that there will be time to explore his ideas.

If the history of your relationship with your child is one of trust and mutual respect, it would seem you have already developed skill in discussing his questions and concerns. The child who senses that a parent always gives honest answers and never offers misleading information eventually turns to that parent for guidance and information. If you are patient, tolerant, and reliable, you are capable of satisfying your child's curiosity; you are an "askable" parent.

Conversely, a parent who has not developed that kind of trust with a child will find it difficult to discuss feelings, and so will the child. Rather than turn to others for answers, some children may attempt to answer their own questions as best they can with the help of their fantasies. Needless to say, this is not a reliable source and can lead a child to a great many erroneous conclusions. In such cases, professional psychological help is of great value. Arrange a consultation with a professional who is sensitive to children and has had experience in such situations.

"My wife and I have discussed our marital difficulties for a long time and have finally agreed that we should divorce. We are on speaking terms and feel amicable toward one another, since we understand each other's reasons for the divorce. My wife wants to break the news to our three children by herself and not with me. I am afraid she will slant her explanation in such a way that the children will feel sympathy for her and anger toward me. I know I can convince her to let us handle the discussion together, but should I, or should I let her do it in her own way?"

When parents are on amicable terms and have agreed to the divorce the way you have, it is best for them to tell the children together. If, however, they are angry, resentful, and filled with self-pity, it's possible that each parent explaining the divorce separately would choose words that would tend to slant things in his or her favor.

I think you should try to convince your wife that you should tell the children together, if for no other reason than to avoid feeling that she is in some way taking advantage of the situation. This suspicion would be bound to cause you to feel resentment toward her and might destroy the amicable relationship you have at present. In handling the initial explanation together, take care that you present your views in such a way that neither of you blames or implies blame on the other. You will each have ample opportunity later on to speak to the children separately and explain your position in more detail. Assure the children that any time they have any questions or concerns they should feel free to come to either of you.

"I think my little four-year-old daughter is all mixed up. I explained very carefully about our decision to live apart from one another and how we both still loved her. One minute she seems to accept my explanation and the next minute asks me when Daddy is coming back. Then in the next breath she starts talking about visiting Daddy in his new home. Her emotions are equally unpredictable. What did I do wrong?"

You didn't necessarily do anything wrong. Your daughter's feelings will fluctuate for quite a while. Do not expect her to have a well-formulated set of ideas. Make sure that she knows you understand her feelings. I recommend you say something like, "I know you may feel all mixed up about things, and that your feelings will change from time to time—they will shift around a lot before you feel sure of yourself." Let her know that this does not mean she is confused, but that she is thinking about what is happening and has to try out different ways of looking at things in order to be more sure of herself and her feelings.

"My niece brags that her child showed no reaction to his parents' sudden announcement of divorce after fourteen years of what seemed like a happy marriage. There must be something wrong for this child to seem so unaffected. How do you explain this?"

Some parents pride themselves on the fact that their children "took it like grown-ups," which means they had no response. No doubt, such a "response" from a child makes the immediate situation easier for the parent. But what's really happening is that all the turmoil is under the surface and the true feelings are not coming out. This calm exterior does not signify that the child is accepting the situation without feeling —you can be sure there will be a delayed reaction.

"I'd rather leave well enough alone. I don't want to upset my child by discussing things he doesn't bring up himself, and I'm too upset to go into details. Am I doing the wrong thing?"

The reluctance on the part of some parents to explore a child's feelings is based on the notion that they must protect the child from the burdens of divorce. Therefore, they shy away from any discussion of the subject. It is absurd to think that by ignoring something, it ceases to exist. I want to say emphatically, you are *not* protecting your son by refusing to discuss his feelings. In fact, by denying him the opportunity of expressing himself, you are leaving him highly vulnerable to feelings of helplessness and defiance. I believe you should talk to your son about the divorce yourself or get professional help —but do one or the other.

"Two weeks ago I told my three children that their mother and I would be getting divorced. I explained that we were not happy together, which they readily understood because of the problems we have been having for a few years. In some ways the news seemed to come as a relief for the children, but at the same time they seemed anxious about what would happen to them. My daughter, who is fifteen, asked if she could live with me, but my other two daughters, ages eight and eleven, want to live with my wife. We agreed to those arrangements, but I didn't tell them that I planned to get married again three weeks from now when all the legal details are completed.

"My children have never met the woman I plan to marry, but she is very friendly, loves children, and is very slim and beautiful—not at all like their mother, who is forty pounds overweight. This woman has a daughter of her own, who will be living with us. For all intents and purposes my new wife will be taking over the role of mother for my fifteen-year-old daughter. I am anxious about telling my children about my remarriage and wonder how they will take to my new wife. What can I do to avoid any problems under these circumstances?"

It seems to me that you are asking an awful lot from your children in a short period of time. Accepting the idea of divorce is, in and of itself, a major problem. Dealing with the transition and disruption in family life requires time, patience, and understanding on everyone's part. Telling your children about your remarriage to someone they don't yet know, and expecting them at the same time to accept another child—

your new wife's daughter—creates an enormous amount of uncertainty and is sure to color their feelings toward you.

There is a greater chance that your children will reject your new wife if your remarriage comes before they have been able to adjust themselves to your divorce. They could easily look upon her as the woman who stole their father away. The fact that she is "slim and very beautiful" and not overweight like their mother might cause them to be sympathetic to their mother and feel that you have abandoned her because of a physical problem. It is not at all unlikely that your wife, who is also unaware of your intended remarriage, will feel jealous and resentful. Clearly these attitudes will be communicated to your children, and will intensify their loyalty toward their mother and increase their resentment toward you.

In my opinion, the circumstances surrounding your divorce and remarriage are extremely delicate and bound to cause many problems. If you could possibly put off your remarriage until your children's lives can be stabilized, they would be far better able to handle the enormous problems ahead of them. Let them get to know the woman you intend to marry over a period of time so that they can adjust to her as your friend before expecting them to accept her as their stepmother. This is particularly important for your fifteen-year-old daughter, who will be living with her, as well as with her own child.

If you move slowly into these various transitions, there is a far greater possibility that things will work out smoothly. Frankly, I believe you and your children should have good psychological counseling during this period.

CHAPTER 3

THE IMPACT ON YOUR CHILD

A CHILD IS bombarded by all kinds of feelings, many of them well below the surface, during the period of divorce. It is not easy for these feelings to come to the surface all at once; nor should they.

Most children have sufficient control and the kind of psychological "safety valves" that enable them to tolerate a certain amount of stress without becoming overwhelmed or disorganized. The one overriding concern a child is sure to have, perhaps more covertly than overtly, is whether anything he did could have caused the breakup of his parents' marriage. In other words, "What did I do to cause this to happen?"

No matter how mature or intelligent the child is, and no matter how much the facts speak otherwise, this question invariably arises, if only for a moment. Younger children, between the ages of two and five, tend to see the world in an egocentric way. In a sense, they feel things are happening because they caused them to happen. For example, a child walking down the street sees the moon in parallax and says, "The moon is following me." During this same developmental stage, a child whose parents have left him in the company of a stranger while he was asleep may interpret the phenomenon as "Going to sleep made my parents go away."

Furthermore, parental arguments frequently center on issues concerning the children. If the parents have argued vehemently in front of the children about issues such as bedtime, the food they eat, school, or anything else that comes up in the normal course of a child's life, that child will feel responsible for the divorce. Generally speaking, whether parents argue about the children in front of them or not, children still question their role in causing the marital breakup.

In a similar vein, a child sometimes overhears statements made in anger, which are then distorted in her mind. A good deal depends upon the age of the child, but generally children under the age of five or six are somewhat literal in their interpretation of what they hear. Conceivably, she may have overheard a parental argument, or perhaps a telephone conversation in which her mother said to a friend, "Oh, I could kill him for that!" While this statement was merely a figure of speech, the child may not understand that, and may fear that her mother is about to kill her father. Moreover, she may feel that she is in a position to either make it happen or to prevent it from happening. She is afraid to intervene and, as a result, may be overwhelmed by anxiety.

I have known some children whose feelings of responsibility and guilt were so strong that they could only get relief by scratching or biting themselves or depriving themselves of some pleasure.

I met periodically with one little eight-year-old, Elizabeth, during the period surrounding her parents' divorce. She reported hearing, hour after hour, her mother's conversations with friends, lawyers, and relatives, in which she spewed forth everything that was on her mind and continually repeated her desire to hurt her husband and get as much money as she could out of him.

Elizabeth had nightmares of her father being attacked by her mother and found herself biting her hand because she felt that by hurting herself she would prevent her father from being hurt. She was deeply frightened by her mother and resentful toward her, but at the same time felt she had to be very nice to her, for if she did not comply with all her mother's wishes and show detachment toward her father she would be unable to prevent the threats from being carried out on him.

Clearly Elizabeth had a terrible burden of responsibility and needed counseling in how to deal with her mother. It was not possible for her to discuss her feelings with her mother, and for this reason special help was of great use. My point in bringing up this example is not only to emphasize the value of professional help, but to show how a child's ruminations about her parents' divorce can be dangerously distorted by chance remarks or exaggerated expressions.

Children do not like to see their parents unhappy. Many children take on the added responsibility of protecting their parents from discomfort, which can, in turn, cause them to hold back their own feelings and problems so as not to overburden their parents. A child might withhold information to avoid hurting a parent or, more often than not, take a protective attitude toward the parent and suffer quietly.

Parents are often so preoccupied with their own feelings during this difficult time that they appear insensitive to the needs of their children. Worry over parental unhappiness can be the most burdensome aspect of a divorce for a child. The child who doesn't want to talk about his feelings or the child who seems to show no reaction may, in fact, simply be trying to protect his parents from any further distress.

As you try to get your child to open up and discuss her feelings, you may be answered with a sad "I don't know," which is a frequent response to searching questions. Feelings are building up that often cannot be discussed with either parent for fear of hurting the other. If your child shows warmth and compassion to you she may fear that your adversary, the other parent, will reject her. By the same token, she may be reluctant to express her anger and resentment toward you for fear that you will reject her. This fear of rejection can overwhelm your child; her suppressed feelings have no outlet, and often symptoms of emotional or physical disturbance develop and may persist for some time.

Ronald was a thirteen-year-old who seemed very much in control during the period of turmoil preceding his parents' divorce, yet he appeared depressed and rarely smiled. He immersed himself in a number of solitary hobbies and had little to say about what was going on in his family. Obviously, he witnessed the discord between his parents, but he singlemindedly followed the responsibilities he set up for himself. He fed his tropical fish regularly, kept their tank clean, and read every book he could get his hands on about the care and behavior of tropical fish. He wanted to make their lives happy.

Ronald identified with the fish and took care of them as

meticulously as he wished his parents would take care of him. He was the "good" parent. When I pointed this out to him in an effort to get him to release his feelings, he answered that he had purposely arranged his life so he wouldn't react. By being calm, he felt he would make things "all right." He truly believed he had an important role to play as a neutralizer in order to keep things balanced; if he let his feelings out, the divorce would be inevitable.

Though superficially Ronald was calm, controlled, and rigid in carrying out his responsibilities, he was basically fearful that one "false move" on his part would split his parents apart forever. His rigid detachment was his way of holding his parents' marriage together.

Some children feel shame when their parents are getting divorced. If the parents are ashamed, the child can easily mirror the parents' feelings. Particularly if the marriage seemed to be a happy one, the unexpected announcement may be accompanied by a sense of shame. Frequently such a divorce arouses gossip in the community: "They seemed like such a happy couple—you would never know anything was wrong." Their playmates sometimes aggravate children's feelings of shame by teasing them about their parents' divorce.

It is important, therefore, to raise the question of shame by asking your child, "Does it make you feel embarrassed when people find out about our divorce?" This might give the child an opening so she can discuss these feelings freely.

In some cases, a parent leaves after the divorce and is not heard from for a long time. The children are then left in a quandary, not knowing why that parent no longer wants to be with them. It is very common for children not only to wonder where that parent is but also to have a compulsive desire to go out and find him or her. "Who is feeding him?"

they wonder. "What will happen to her if she gets sick?" "Why doesn't he write to us, or call us?" As you can see, these concerns are upsetting, and the uncertainty they produce in the child's life can be very disconcerting. While a parent who has abandoned a family may have spared everyone the anger and fighting, he has left behind a situation which can at times be far more disorganizing than dealing with open hostility.

I am increasingly convinced that not *all* children love their parents, in spite of the pressures to do so. Strangely enough, we accept the fact that people go into psychiatric treatment in an attempt to work through their angry feelings toward their parents, yet when speaking of the trauma of divorce, invariably people will insist that children suffer because they are being torn apart by their love for both parents. Sometimes divorce helps a child come to terms with his true feelings about a parent. One parent may, in fact, be a tyrant, and the child was terrified of that parent while the marriage lasted. If the tyrannical behavior contributed to the divorce, the child has a sense of relief and affirmation that he is not alone with these feelings. While this is not a common occurrence, I simply want to point out that possibility in the course of re-examining all our conventional thinking about divorce and its impact on the child.

I recently saw Susan, a twelve-year-old who felt responsible for her father's happiness after the divorce of her parents. She felt terribly sorry for him, and always wondered how he managed now that he lived alone. She found herself trying to please him, even though she did not necessarily want to do the things she knew would please him. Eventually she found herself resenting him and wanting to pull away from him. She had her own feelings about both her father and her mother, but no one really asked, nor made it easy for her to express those feelings. Her father would call her many times during the day simply to say to her, "Susan, I love you, I just wanted you to know." He would check in every morning before she went to school with a similar call. She began to dread the ring of the telephone.

In talking with Susan and exploring her feelings I found that she felt the obligation to answer her father with "I love you too," yet she could not bring herself to say it. Her resentment increased until it built up to the point where she asked for outside help, and I became her therapist. She admitted quite readily to me that she was afraid to hurt her father's feelings. She explained that in some ways he tried to get her to feel sorry for him—he was the kind of man that always did everything anyone else wanted, but never did what he wanted. She resented this behavior deeply, and she raised her voice in anger as she said, "He never gave anyone else the satisfaction of doing what *he* wanted, so *we* could be nice to him for a change. When someone asked him what he wanted to do he would say, 'It doesn't matter.' He was always perfect—no one could ever criticize him. All he did was sacrifice for us."

This unhappy twelve-year-old needed to unload her feelings and frustrations, and wanted me to intervene to get her father off her back. She resented his sacrificing nature and, as hard as it was, finally confessed that she wasn't sure she really loved him. As far back as she could remember she felt this way, but since everyone expected her to love her father she could never admit these feelings. Once her resentment was expressed, Susan seemed more relaxed, her school performance improved, and she became more sociable with her friends.

Children need to be heard in most of life's situations; it is imperative that they be heard during the difficult time when a divorce is taking place. If you want to minimize the

negative impact of divorce on your child, you have to prepare yourself for whatever feelings your child may want to
express, some of which may be upsetting to you.

When a child is left in a situation of great uncertainty he
may feel so helpless and frustrated and angry that his only
relief comes with direct expressions of aggression and destructiveness. Many children are quick to engage in fights
with peers and are generally antagonistic. Vandalism is not
uncommon among children who feel the adult world is
mistreating them and denying them the happiness they
desperately want.

Thirteen-year-old Jeff was a star athlete and well liked by
his teachers and coaches in school. He was caught by the
police one night breaking windows in his neighborhood.
His parents were shocked at this totally "out of character"
behavior and, desperate, turned to me for assistance. What
his mother described to me was clearly an ongoing family
breakup in which Jeff was ignored. When I later spoke with
Jeff alone, he confirmed my impression of his family. "My
parents are only concerned about themselves and money.
No one gives a hoot for how I feel. I've had enough of it!
I'm mad—I'd like to run away or burn the house down. *Now*
they are upset because I broke some windows. I'm glad
they're upset—maybe they'll pay attention to me and how
I feel, for a change."

Jeff's vandalism not only served as a release for his feelings, but he also got back at his parents, and managed to
focus on what he needed in the first place—concern for *his*
feelings.

A multitude of physical symptoms can accompany the
psychological states I've been discussing. Sleeplessness or
fitful sleep is a symptom many parents describe in their
children during the period surrounding a divorce. One
child summed up his feelings by saying to me, "I don't

know what is going to happen. I'm afraid I am going to be left alone. I wake up to see if someone's there, or if they left me." The sleeplessness occurs more frequently during the times when anxiety is heightened. His apprehension is understandable; he doesn't know from day to day what is going to happen or where he is going to live. In my observations, this fear subsides when living arrangements are worked out.

Any kind of mental activity is a strain during the turmoil of divorce. All children attempt to work out their problems through fantasies, dreams, and play. Their preoccupation with the "unsolvable" problems in their life drains their mental energy. It is common for children in the stressful situation of a divorce to have difficulty concentrating, and teachers frequently complain of their daydreaming in class.

Another symptom that occurs frequently is crying. These episodes can occur sporadically throughout the day and during wakeful periods at night, and can sometimes be overwhelming to a child. While it is good to release these feelings, it is still confusing to the child. "I don't know why I am crying, I am just sad," she will say. Pressing her by asking, "Why are you crying?" simply makes things worse. There is usually no specific reason, and she is correct in saying she doesn't know why she is crying.

Muscle weakness or physical exhaustion is a frequent complaint in young children under the stress of divorce. Their emotional state is reflected in feelings of physical exhaustion, and their muscle weakness relates to feelings of helplessness. It is as if the body has complied with the child's emotional state; he is essentially immobilized by the circumstances.

A lack of appetite, complaints of stomachaches, and a sad facial expression also reflect a child's generalized depression, caused by feelings of loss. While neither parent has actually been lost, as is the case with the death of a parent, the child is reacting to the impending "loss" of his family as he has grown to know it.

A child's attitude about himself affects the way he walks, the way he eats, and the way he takes care of himself in general. An unhappy child looks unkempt and frequently develops a sallow color. He does not smile easily and can break into tears at the smallest criticism. He wonders what is going to happen but is afraid to ask, for fear of being ignored and feeling unimportant.

I am convinced that the feeling of helplessness weakens a child's defenses against all kinds of stress, both emotional and physical. For this reason these children are more highly susceptible to infections and illnesses in general. This is true for all depressed people.

Though these physical symptoms can be caused by the stress of divorce, it is essential that parents have their children checked by a physician to make sure that the complaints are not caused by organic disease. If the symptoms persist and the child is immobilized, unable to function in school or with his friends, professional help should be sought.

As I mentioned earlier, it is sometimes far easier for a child to release his feelings to a professional outside his family. The child must be assured that this person is there to help him and will keep his conversations confidential. Children frequently want to keep the content of their conversations private, even from their parents.

Not every child requires professional help, since many children have the strength, in conjunction with parental support, to come through a divorce psychologically intact. Some parents are quick to get professional help at the first signs of discomfort. I hesitate to recommend counseling or psychotherapy at such a time, since I firmly believe that unnecessary treatment can sometimes be as damaging as not seeking treatment at all when the circumstances warrant it. In the course of any child's life there will be difficult periods which tax all her emotional resources. I'm impressed with how well many children do emerge from extremely traumatic situations. These children invariably had parents who from early infancy onward helped them develop resources for coping with stress.

The following are some of the questions and responses to problems that have arisen in my consultation with patients concerning the impact of divorce on children.

"During my marriage my husband worked long hours and was frequently away on business trips. Consequently my son, who is now ten, and I spent a lot of time together. Even though he seemed glad to see his father when he was at home, I always sensed in him a little jealousy and resentment toward his father. Now that we are divorced, my son hovers over me, worries about me if I am not constantly smiling, and reassures me that he will take care of me so that I'll have nothing to worry about. He even said, 'Don't worry, Mom, I'll be like a husband to you.'

"I am a little concerned about him, even though it's nice to have his support and reassurance. I get the feeling that he is happy about our divorce, since it gives him an opportunity to actually take his father's place. I have heard of the term 'Oedipus complex' and wonder if my child is having this kind of problem. I also wonder, should I encourage his behavior or discourage it?"

It doesn't matter what term you use to describe the configuration of your son's relationship with you, although it does have many of the classic features of the Oedipus complex. It seems to me that he is missing out on his childhood, taking on an adult role, which makes me seriously concerned about the possibility of significant psychological problems in the future.

During your marriage your son exhibited some of the typical jealousies a young boy shows toward his father, which frequently lend themselves to a competitive struggle with the father for the mother's affections. In the process of this "normal" struggle, a young boy takes on many of the father's characteristics and in a sense establishes his own sexual indentification through an identification with him.

If the father, as in your case, is absent a good deal of the time or is weak and ineffectual, it is more difficult for a child to establish a clear-cut sexual identification. By literally having the mother to himself, a child may see himself in the role of "husband," and in some cases, even as the mother's "lover."

A boy in this situation frequently has adultlike characteristics and may be the kind of "goody-goody" child that many adults admire for being so "grown-up" and responsible. But in his role as "husband," the child is vulnerable to a great deal of sexual conflict. Here he is in a close relationship with his mother, and what is he to do with his sexual impulses and fantasies? How can he live with incestuous thoughts? While these thoughts may not be on the surface, they exist in the unconscious mind with such intensity that he has to develop defenses and behavior patterns to enable him to live comfortably with his mother without the threat of having his sexual impulses emerge.

A child should not be encouraged to take on the role of a "husband" under any circumstances, whether in an intact marriage or after a divorce. As important as it is for children to have strong family ties, it's equally important that they have peer relationships and relationships with other people that are geared to their age level. At the same time, do not be harsh with your son if he expresses a wish to take care of you. Simply make it clear that he is not your husband but your son, and encourage behavior that is consistent with that relationship.

In many instances psychological help is not necessary for the child who is involved in this type of family situation. But bear in mind that your child, even during his early years of life, had sexual impulses toward you, which in a sense was condoned rather than opposed by you and your husband. At the present time you and your son are living in an arrangement which represents the fulfillment of an unconscious wish—that he be alone with his mother. In all likelihood, he feels some degree of guilt; it's as if his wishes came true and he is therefore responsible for the divorce. I would strongly recommend that you take your son to a child psychiatrist or child psychologist for counseling because I feel he could benefit from talking with someone outside his immediate family.

"The uncertainty in our situation is terrible, and our settlement is still up in the air. My wife has changed lawyers four times and we keep getting delays from the court for our divorce hearing. My son has become very bossy and wants to control everything and everyone. It seems to get worse from day to day and now he has become preoccupied—even possessed—by remote-control devices. He has a hunger for information on all the mechanisms for controlling things in outer space and on other planets, as well as missiles and various mechanical devices. His favorite toy is a model boat which has a remote-control mechanism. I don't understand this change in his personality. I am very confused. Is it a sign of a nervous breakdown? Why is it so intense?

In this terrible period of uncertainty, I am sure your greatest desire is to get your life under control once again and eliminate the present agony. In a sense, you are hanging in a state of suspended animation, and the uncertainty prevents you from making any plans for the future. One of the most excruciating aspects of a divorce is the waiting without knowing the outcome. You feel "I don't care how it turns out as long as I *know!*" Your son is experiencing the same feeling. He attempts to deal with the uncertainty and master the anxiety it creates by taking control of "everything" and "everyone."

In psychological terms, your son has displaced his need to take control of his life into controlling objects. The more he can learn about dictating the behavior of complicated and possibly dangerous objects, the more he will feel a sense of inner strength. It's as if he is saying to himself, "I can't stand feeling so powerless in the face of all the uncertainties in my life—I want to be in control so I can make things happen myself." By being in control of his model boat and making it do what he wants, he creates some semblance of mastery over events in his life. Those massive worlds in outer space, those strange objects on other planets, and those dangerous missiles in a sense represent the uncontrollable and potentially explosive elements of his life during this time of turmoil in his family.

"My five-year-old daughter becomes hysterical whenever I scold her about her behavior. Unfortunately, she has overheard some of the angry fights between my husband and me and was in the house the night I exploded at my husband, said that I could no longer put up with him, and threw him out of the house. Now my daughter is terrified that I will kick her out of the house if she misbehaves. I know it's logical for a child to think this way and it certainly makes a lot of sense, but how can I assure her that the same thing won't happen with her?"

Explain to your daughter that you love her even when she misbehaves. Let her know that though you may get angry when she does certain things, this in no way means you could ever think of kicking her out of the house. Explain that the feelings parents have toward children are very different from the kinds of feelings they have toward each other. To illustrate your point, explain how all living things, including animals, are very protective of their children, and will often sacrifice their own lives to protect them. Assure her that there is a special kind of relationship between the two of you that will always keep you close together even though you may get angry with her from time to time.

Try your best to avoid using expressions in anger that might be taken literally, such as "I've had enough! I can't stand it any longer," or "If you do that again, I'll never forgive you." Such extreme statements can easily be interpreted by your child as proof of your intention to abandon her. As time goes on, your daughter will be able to interpret your expressions of annoyance or anger more realistically, and her fear of being kicked out of the house will most likely recede.

"After my wife picked up and decided she was going to try a new life style on her own, my eight-year-old son and I seem to have gotten our lives together and are very happy. He rarely sees his mother because she is 2,500 miles away, although she writes and telephones occasionally. He obviously misses her from time to time and asks a lot of questions about why she left. I have explained that she was unhappy and felt she had to live someplace else to find a way of becoming happy.

"My son is doing well in school, has many friends, and everyone finds him delightful. Recently, however, he has become very serious and protective toward me and constantly warns me to be careful crossing the street and to drive slowly. He becomes noticeably upset if I am five minutes late coming home. I hate seeing him so worried and upset and wonder why he has become so filled with anxiety."

Children can become preoccupied with fantasies of terrible things happening to their parents because of an underlying hostility toward them. They are frightened by their own angry feelings—after all, the fantasy originated in the child's mind and in a sense represents the child's wish. The anxiety comes from the fear that it might come true, and the child then expresses an overprotective attitude toward the parent.

However, in your son's case, it sounds as if he wants to take good care of what is left of his emotional security. His mother left him and you to find happiness elsewhere. It's logical for him to wonder if perhaps you might do the same and leave him completely alone. His anxiety is probably increased by his awareness of some of the realities of life; people *do* get hit by cars while crossing the street and get injured in accidents. Coming home late may mean that something has happened to you; consequently, he worries that he might lose his remaining parent, the only person offering him the security and love he needs.

While all children have some fear of abandonment by parents, children of divorce are more vulnerable to this problem. Their anxiety about abandonment can make them fear to take any steps toward their own independence because they see independence as an abandonment of their parents. At this time your son needs reassurance of your love for him and your promise to be very careful about yourself. In all likelihood his fears will diminish as his life stabilizes, but if they don't, professional psychological help should be made available to him. In my experience, children with this problem generally do well in short-term psychotherapy.

"I am a schoolteacher who has witnessed the effects of divorce on children through their classroom behavior and I am very puzzled. There seems to be no clear-cut pattern when it comes to their reactions in the classroom. In fact, some children seem to work harder and get better grades when their parents are on the threshold of divorce, while others seem to come apart completely and lose all motivation. Some make themselves so obnoxious that other children tease them and treat them like scapegoats, while others defy all authority and constantly draw attention to themselves through their problem behavior. I keep hearing the term 'children of divorce' and have always assumed that there is a clear-cut pattern that makes these children different from all other children. Why are they all so different while they are going through the same kind of problem?''

Not all people react to a given stress in the same way. In fact, each person has a unique pattern of response to stress situations. This fact was established by Dr. Hans Selye, who is internationally renowned for his studies on stress. Dr. Selye also found that when stress exists over a prolonged period of time, both the psychological and physical mechanisms in the body undergo changes depending upon the individual's capacity to come to terms with the stressor agent (that which causes the stress).

The different reactions you have observed in children reflect variations in their personalities, their previous experiences, the emotional resources of their families, and the specific circumstances surrounding the divorce in their particular families. The child who works harder and gets better grades may be trying to establish a sense of mastery over his life. Perhaps he feels in some magical way that achieving success in his academic life will give him the omnipotence for willing success in his personal life. His academic achievements are his way of undoing the failure of his parents' marriage.

The children you have observed who lose motivation may be reacting to their feelings of hopelessness and helplessness. These children may have given up simply because they feel no one cares about them. Those who constantly get in trouble may be retaliating against their parents indirectly, or may be trying to gain their attention in a negative way if they feel they are being ignored. Those children who bully are generally frightened inside and overwhelmed by the power others have over them. By bullying others they gain a false sense of power, and are attempting to guard against being overpowered by others instead.

It is obvious from your observations that there is no single pattern that characterizes the emotional reactions of children of divorce. I am sure you have seen these very same reactions in many children whose families are intact.

CHAPTER 4

PRESERVING YOUR CHILD'S INTEGRITY

WHEN TWO PEOPLE create a human life as a result of their relationship, they do not own that life. In a sense, that life belongs to the world. Children are the true victims of divorce, yet their role in divorce has traditionally been ignored. At most, their needs and welfare have been given lip service.

The conventional legal definition of "child" provides insight into our view of children. In many states a child under twenty-one is referred to as an "infant child." "Children of tender years" is a term used frequently to refer to children under fourteen. In the various legal documents necessary to file for a divorce, children are referred to as "issues of the marriage." Undeniably, the language we use reflects the real meaning we are trying to convey. From these terms alone it seems clear that young people are regarded as infantile, painfully fragile, and essentially products of the marriage, rather than as human beings with definite needs and desires.

The defining of children in these terms suggests that they are incapable of independent dealings and require a kind of psychological swaddling to protect them from any involvement in the reorganization of their lives. Yet parents expect their children to sleep in total darkness at a young age, and consider it a weakness if a five-year-old feels more comfortable with a night light on. If a child clings to infantile patterns such as thumb sucking, carrying around a security blanket, or insisting on having a cuddly animal beside him at night, or shows some reluctance to separate from a parent on the first day of school beyond the age of three, his behavior is considered immature and inappropriate.

We expect a child to be able to make decisions and to show independence and responsibility during these so-called tender years. From the first day of school children are expected to socialize in a peer group situation. They are given homework from the first grade on. They are expected to handle their share of household chores and responsibilities on a regular basis. These legally helpless creatures described as "infant children" are expected to travel on buses to and from school and to move around in a city without adult supervision.

Parents frequently consult me because of their children's so-called infantile or immature behavior and want help in guiding them toward greater independence and self-sufficiency during the early childhood years. Without belaboring the subject, I simply want to point out the incongruity between the legal concept of a child and parental and societal expectations. It is precisely this incongruity, and the failure to recognize the importance of building self-esteem through child-rearing practices, that set a climate for disregarding a child's integrity.

Parents and professionals react favorably when I urge and instruct them to give children options that allow them some participation in the outcome of a traumatic event, such as a hospital stay. No one quarrels with the idea that we should be honest with children in preparing them for what will take place during a physical examination, a medical procedure, or a stay in the hospital, yet when divorce is imminent, we are reluctant to let our children participate. Children become depressed, uncooperative, or defiant when they are unprepared or misled by health professionals. Understandably, if they are apprehensive they'll be more vulnerable to pain. Children want and need to participate to some degree in the decisions affecting their lives. Children with chronic diseases or children who have to undergo serious medical procedures such as transplants, open heart surgery, or periodic blood transfusions come away stronger and with a greater sense of mastery over these stressful situations if they have dealt with their feelings beforehand. The key to success in handling these problems is having responsible adults, respectful of the child's feelings and wishes, who prepare them for what is going to happen and who give them options whenever possible. When I speak of options for the child who needs a blood transfusion, I do not mean the choice of having or not having the transfusion; I mean giving the child an option as to which arm should receive the transfusion. Similarly, the child recovering from a lifesaving organ transplant needs to have options regarding various daily procedures. "Would you like to walk to the X-ray room or would you like a wheelchair?" "Would you like me to change your bandages now, or an hour from now?" This gives the young patient an opportunity to exercise some control over his life. In my experience a doctor or nurse who frequently visits the child and asks, "Can I make you more comfortable in some way, like lowering or raising your bed?" gives that child a small yet important choice in a situation where he is so very dependent on others for his welfare.

Doctors who are most sympathetic to the wishes and feelings of their patients find that those patients make the best recoveries. I feel that the role of parents during the unpleasant procedure of divorce is somewhat parallel to the role of doctors during a medical emergency: if parents are sympathetic to the wishes and feelings of their children and let them participate in the decisions about their future, the children will be far less likely to experience the emotional trauma of distress, defiance, depression, guilt, and anxiety.

Parents who are divorcing must approach the matter of their child's wishes and feelings cautiously to avoid placing her in a position where she is asked to choose the parent she loves the most. In most cases a child has love for both parents and wants a continuing relationship with them. Difficult though it is, you can convey to a child that by expressing her wishes as to where and with whom she would prefer to live, this choice does not imply rejection of one parent in favor of the other. It is absolutely essential for the parents to explain to her that "we both love you no matter which of us you prefer to live with." With this assurance the child will be able to express herself more readily, with a minimal feeling of guilt about rejecting the other parent. A sufficiently mature parent is able to recognize that a child may prefer one parent's life style over the other's and, assuming both life styles meet the requirements of being a responsible parent, the child's choice should be looked upon with respect.

I do *not* believe the ultimate choice should be left up to the child. The determination should be made by the judge, a court-appointed advocate for the child, or lawyers working in concert with each other to facilitate the best possible arrangement in conformity with the child's wishes. Make it clear to the child that she will *not* make the choice. Explain that the choice will be made by others, who will take all factors into consideration, including her own wishes.

It is unquestionably difficult to place infants and toddlers into a situation where their choice plays a role. Nevertheless, it is possible to evaluate their reactions to their parents. To illustrate the point, a study was conducted to evaluate the differences in infants' reactions to their mothers and their fathers. A number of eighteen-month-olds were observed in a setting where both parents were present. When a stranger entered the room the infants showed a preference for turning toward their mothers. On the other hand, in a free-play situation without the presence of a stranger, the infants showed a powerful preference for the fathers, as evidenced by the display of smiling, vocalizing, looking, and attempting to engage them in play activities. These findings not only challenge the "mystique of motherhood" but demonstrate that it is possible to evaluate preferences of infants. The notion that infants and toddlers are automatically better off with mothers has no scientific validity.

In my own observations of toddlers and their parents I see reactions that reflect the child's sense of security with each of them. Frequently there is a significant difference in these reactions which helps me to judge a child's feelings. When a child is verbal it's easier to determine which parent seems to provide him with greater emotional security. The process of getting children to express their feelings is too complex to reduce to a simple formula, but one example of my approach involves probing into the child's emotions in various situations: "Do you ever get scared?" "When?" "What frightens you?" "What makes you feel comfortable?" "Why do you like being with your mother?" I try to approach these areas of inquiry from all angles in the least threatening way possible. The child's answers are not the only indication of what is significant or revealing; sometimes physical reactions, more than words, reflect his deepest wishes and feelings.

Obviously, as children grow older they are more capable of articulating their feelings. It is important not only to explore how a child feels about such matters as with which parent he will live, but also to understand his reasons for making that choice.

Recently a divorced mother with custody of her two children called to talk to me about her ten-year-old daughter, Jennifer, who suddenly started having problems in school. Her teachers were concerned that she was not doing her work, making only enough effort to get by, and was beginning to show defiance to authority. She fought with other children, was generally irritable, and was increasingly sloppy in the way she dressed. Prior to this, she had been a relatively good student, was popular with her friends, and showed only occasional moodiness. She had had some difficult episodes, but they were short-lived and sporadic. Now the situation seemed far more serious.

In describing the circumstances of Jennifer's life, her mother indicated that she was rather close to her father and always looked forward to visiting him. She saw him once during the week and every other weekend. The mother admitted that the father was a warm man who shared many activities with his daughter and that they had a very good relationship. As she discussed her own relationship with

Jennifer, she described her impatience with her daughter and confessed that she lost her temper from time to time because of her defiance. The mother mentioned that despite her bad moods, Jennifer was extremely self-sufficient and could be relied upon to carry out her responsibilities.

The mother felt something was wrong with her daughter but couldn't pinpoint the problem. She recognized that matters had grown worse when she began dating a man, whom she was considering marrying. "Things were difficult before, but this apparently didn't help matters," she said. She admitted that this man was not especially "child-oriented" but he liked her children and was nice to them.

Before discussing the details of her problems, after interviewing her mother, I met with Jennifer. I assured Jennifer that our talks would be confidential and that I would not discuss anything with her parents that she did not wish me to talk about.

Jennifer was an average ten-year-old who spoke with confidence and without hesitation. I asked her if she knew why her mother brought her to me and she said, "Yes, I am having trouble with my school work." She was very forthright in making this statement and went on to say, "My mother and I don't get along. She doesn't understand me, and she loses patience with me. We rarely enjoy doing things together, even though she tries."

I asked Jennifer how she felt about coming to see me and she said, "I wanted to come because I hope that you can help me." I asked her what she meant and she said, "You would do me the biggest favor in the world and make me the happiest person if you could make my mother understand how I feel. I know all my problems would go away if I could live with my father. My mother told me I can't do that until I'm older. I can't wait that long. I am very unhappy. I know what I want and I think she knows what I want, and that's why she keeps telling me I can't live with my father. I hate her for it and wish she would understand. My father has a lot of patience with me. He really understands me and we have a lot of fun together. When I get sick he believes me, but my mother thinks I am faking. I really wish you could do something about it. *I know* all my problems would go away if I could live with my father."

I arranged to meet with both of Jennifer's parents. It was obvious that they had some differences of opinion, but basically they were able to speak with each other in a relatively friendly manner, and both claimed that they were genuinely interested in helping Jennifer. I told them that I had given Jennifer some psychological tests and she appeared to be a relatively stable, emotionally healthy child, who was not a problem child but a child with problems.

Her parents expressed sufficient trust in me to ask my opinion about how to help Jennifer. I explained that what I was about to tell them might be somewhat distressing but I wanted to be as direct as possible. I said that Jennifer was sensitive and intelligent, and seemed not only to know what she wanted but understood the source of her problems. In fact, I said, she had asked me to help her solve her problems by interceding on her behalf. I explained that Jennifer said she would be much happier if she could live with her father and visit her mother, and that she felt very strongly about this and thought that all her problems would subside if this wish could be granted. Her mother said, "This doesn't surprise me." They agreed to follow whatever recommendations I made, since they truly wanted Jennifer to be a happy child.

Although her mother looked sad, she obviously understood the importance of Jennifer's decision. She said, "I guess the best way to keep children sometimes is to let them go." She was absolutely right. She recognized the need to respect Jennifer's wishes.

While Jennifer waited in the next room, her parents and I discussed the specific details for changing the living arrangements in an atmosphere of cooperation. Our next concern was Jennifer's younger sister, Amy. Both parents agreed to tell Amy that Jennifer wanted to live with her father now and visit her mother and if Amy wanted to do the same thing, she could. I cautioned them not to put any pressure on Amy, but to explain that she might like to try this arrangement for a while, and if she didn't like it she didn't have to continue it. It was important for her to feel that she too had some choice and that she was being neither abandoned by Jennifer nor pressured into doing what Jennifer was doing.

I then discussed with the parents how they wanted to let Jennifer know of the decision we had reached. They agreed that it might be best for me to call her in and tell her myself in the presence of her parents. When Jennifer came in, she placed herself quite spontaneously on the couch between her parents. I told her that both parents loved her a great deal and truly wanted her to be happy. I explained that we had talked about the situation and that her parents respected her wishes and had agreed to let her live with her father. Jennifer immediately grabbed her mother and put her arms around her, shouting with joy, "Oh, Mommy, thank you so much for being so nice!" She reached over to her father as well and expressed her pleasure at the decision.

Jennifer's happiness with her mother was apparent. There was no resentment, no guilt. The rest of our session involved a very relaxed and casual conversation about the details of when the new arrangement would begin, how Amy would be told, and how Jennifer felt about what Amy might do. Jennifer said, "I would be happy if Amy were with me all the time, but I wouldn't want her to feel that she had to do it just because I am doing it."

I had the clear impression that three relieved and happy people walked out of my office. I think each of them in their own way recognized the feelings of the others, and understood that this was a sensible arrangement under the circumstances. I agreed to see them again periodically, if they so desired, and would be available to help with any problems they might like to discuss with me.

The resentment that children feel toward a parent shows itself in retaliatory ways. Jennifer's difficulty at school, her defiance toward her mother, and all the other manifestations of being a "problem child" were responses to her frustration over being a child with a problem—but, happily, a problem that had a solution.

If you do not respect the integrity of your child, you can be sure he will either internalize your attitude by showing very low self-esteem—that is, by losing respect for his own integrity—or will fight for his integrity if you ignore his wishes. These are the basic patterns that children establish when parents ignore their needs and wishes.

Let me describe twelve-year-old Billy, who was caught in the crossfire between two angry parents. The divorce had taken place two years before, but his parents had continued to sustain a relationship with each other based upon mutual dislike and vindictiveness. The father, who was an avid golfer, had remarried. The mother was a compulsive shopper and had an intense relationship with a man who was not family-oriented.

Billy didn't spend much time with either of his parents, because each was busy with his and her own interests. This, incidentally, was not very different from the way things had been when his parents were together. In fact, there are many intact families where parents spend little time with their children, primarily offering no more than custodial care while pursuing their own interests. Billy's parents, who seemed superficially concerned about his welfare, were no more or less involved in their child's life than many busy parents in continuing marriages.

Billy was successful in making friends among his peers, and was also well liked by adults. He spent most of his time in other people's homes or with his friends. He went home only to eat and sleep, and had managed to build a fairly satisfying life for himself among his friends. Fortunately, these friends were fairly stable youngsters whose values did not include committing destructive acts against themselves or society. I say "fortunately" because Billy was the kind of youngster who would be highly vulnerable to identifying. with the values of any peer group, since his own family was so weak in providing him with the recognition he needed. Whenever Billy visited, his father took him along to the golf course and tried to get him to play with him. Billy had little interest in golf and always managed to find an excuse to do something else. His father was simply putting in time with his son. These visits were unpleasant, but Billy couldn't extricate himself because they were required of him under the divorce agreement.

Nothing in his life in any way nurtured a feeling of love in Billy for either of his parents, and his resentment increased as time went on. Finally his problems showed up through acts of vandalism in the community, which he conducted alone, not with his friends. He began failing subjects in school, and the school authorities called both parents in for a conference. Billy forced his parents into a situation of concern through his vandalism and poor school performance. They had ignored him before, but they couldn't ignore him now.

The conference with the school officials was a fiasco. The

parents argued with each other, and the school principal became the equivalent of a referee in a boxing match. He decided to refer the family for professional help. They consulted me, and I agreed to speak to Billy.

Billy made it clear that he felt angry toward both his parents and thought they never really cared about his wishes and feelings. He resented visiting his father and forced himself to become deaf to his mother's criticisms of his father. He simply wanted to enjoy his friends and not be forced into visits to his father when he had other, more pleasurable things to do.

In the time we had together it became increasingly clear to me that Billy felt insignificant. He wondered why his father insisted on having him visit in accordance with the divorce agreement, even though neither one enjoyed the visits. As we discussed this, he realized that his father was in some way trying to get back at his mother, and he felt that he was being used as a pawn. In further conversation Billy said he would like to work out their times together so that they were mutually agreeable. He resented having his life parceled out into visiting sessions. He was sure he could arrange to visit his father at times that would not interfere with his being with his friends and doing the things he wanted. He admitted that basically he enjoyed being with his friends more than with his father, but was sure he would enjoy the visits more if he went of his own free will. This was arranged, and Billy's adjustment to both his parents improved enormously.

Once Billy became substantially more independent he could no longer be used as a pawn. His independence increased his status in his father's eyes, and caused him to be treated with more respect. The subsequent adjustment made for a much happier youngster.

Even children with emotional problems can handle divorce. However, they need additional support and may require a more concerted effort from those adults arranging the details of the divorce. These children also need to participate in working out the arrangements so that their needs and wishes are taken into consideration, although they will understandably find a divorce much more stressful than will a child with ample emotional resources. You simply have to be more cautious and offer as much emotional support as the situation demands. Be responsive to your child and his emotional needs. Allow him to express his reactions and give him as much structure as you can in helping him see the future with as little ambiguity as possible.

In my years of experience with children in various crisis situations, I have found that those whose parents helped them to develop their own resources in coping with the challenges of everyday life became children who were best equipped to handle the uncertainties of life that occur later on. Whether the challenge be reaching for an object placed in front of a four-month-old child, or coping with that first day away from home in nursery school, or dealing with an overbearing teacher, the child who learns to handle these situations by using his own resources is far more able to deal with any of life's challenges. Divorce is one of those challenges. In fact, the more resourceful child, the one who has gained a sense of mastery in overcoming obstacles, usually comes away from stressful situations stronger than he was before.

Obviously, I am not recommending divorce as a way of strengthening your child's emotional resources, but I do want to point out something I have seen over and over again. Many children who have endured a divorce situation turn out stronger and more emotionally healthy than other children whose parents continue in a bad marriage. Generally speaking, these children have parents who respected their integrity and provided the emotional security that enabled them to surmount crisis situations.

Among the many questions and responses that have arisen in my professional consultations with patients concerning the integrity of their children during divorce are the following:

"I know my daughter feels differently toward my husband than she does toward me. When she seems friendlier toward him, I resent it and think, 'If she's going to belong to him, let him worry about her and take care of her. She's not mine!' I'm having trouble accepting the fact that she may not love both of us equally. Should she?"

The feelings your child has toward you and your spouse are qualitatively different because each of you is a different person. There may also be a quantitative difference, which many people are unwilling to admit. Everyone would like to believe that all children love both parents equally, but this is not the case. Because of this expectation, children are reluctant to admit that they have greater love for one parent than for the other. To acknowledge this fact is virtually taboo. Children are generally expected to express equal love for both parents, and it is precisely this expectation that can cause serious problems for a child when their parents' marriage is coming apart.

Let me emphasize once again that your child, while the product of your marriage, is a person in his or her own right, and not to be regarded as a possession of either parent. The responsibility and the *obligation* of both parents is to provide the optimal conditions for the healthy emotional and physical growth of that child, until he or she is independent. That is the price for bringing a child into the world.

"My divorce is taking a tremendous amount of time and is draining me psychologically. In my new uncertain circumstances, I know it will be hard to fit my life and my children's lives together; I wonder if boarding school and summer camp would be a better arrangement than having them share the struggles I know I am going to have. They are not happy about this, because they have enjoyed living at home and have not even wanted to go off to camp during summer vacations. What should I do?"

During a divorce and for some time afterward, children fear being abandoned by their parents. They often feel that they are in the way and a burden. Sending them away at such a time can serve to confirm their fears and cause them to react like abandoned children, even though your motive is to protect them from the struggles you are undergoing. In my experience I have found that children who remain physically close to home and family during a period of crisis or struggle come away with a greater feeling of family unity than children who have been sent away in order to protect them from upset. Children are resilient and sufficiently sensitive to perceive that they are important to you if you treat them accordingly.

The fact is that many parents do send their children away to camp and boarding school not to protect them but because they *are* a burden. I don't mean to imply that these facilities are dumping grounds for children, but I think it is important for you to realize that some boarding schools are, in fact, a haven for children from families in distress. Sending your child to school or camp with other children who may be experiencing problems does not lighten his emotional load; it actually increases his problems. All things being equal, I truly believe that it is better for a child to be close to his family during a crisis, and have his own needs met by sensitive and concerned family members, than it is to send him off into an environment with people with whom he has had no previous emotional ties.

"My lawyer tells me, 'I can't let an eleven-year-old child run this case!' This is his response every time I bring up the question of my daughter and the problems she's having as we go through the divorce. I tell him my daughter's feelings are at stake and I can't ignore them. She's having a tough time getting along with anyone, doesn't do any school work, and has reverted to all her outgrown habits and fears. My instincts tell me that if her feelings and wishes were considered important as we work out the details of the divorce, she would be a lot better off.

"I need to know your professional view in order to know how to deal with my lawyer and his contention that we have to forget about my daughter's wishes and get on with the legal details of the divorce."

Your instincts are correct. If your child's feelings have not been explored and respected, it is understandable that she has developed a feeling of helplessness. She wonders whether her parents even care for her, let alone love her. Anyone who is subjected to a major change in his life without being consulted on the matter understandably experiences irritation, a feeling of unimportance, and defiance and resentment. His motivation is impaired, morale is negatively affected, and depression takes over. It is important for everyone's sense of self-esteem to participate in decisions that affect their future. The same principle applies to many aspects of child/parent relationships. In my practice as a psychologist I have never seen a patient with destructive or delinquent behavior who did not harbor some underlying wish to retaliate against an authority that refused to hear him or respect his feelings.

Your daughter is obviously having a difficult time coping with your impending divorce. Your job as a parent is to help her mobilize her resources in dealing with this stressful situation. As a start, you must recognize her wishes, take them into consideration, and let her know you care deeply about her and her feelings. Inform your lawyer that your daughter is an integral part of the case and you insist that she be respected as a person.

CHAPTER 5

THE OTHER PEOPLE IN YOUR DIVORCE

DURING THE YEARS of your marriage your relationships with other people were always based on the understanding that you were a married individual. In subtle ways this influenced the quality and nature of how you related to other people. Regardless of the statistics on divorce, when you are married most people assume you will stay married. When you inform them that you have decided to divorce, these people often seem shocked and generally don't know what to say. When you tell an acquaintance that you have just gotten married, you receive a conventional "Congratulations" or "Best wishes" or "I am so happy for you." The fact that society provides no conventional response to the statement that you are about to be divorced is suggestive of the kind of confusion this news causes other people.

Although you may actually be happy about your impending divorce, I think you would be surprised if someone said, "Oh, how wonderful—now you will have the chance to build a life of your own!" Your friends will more likely respond with, "Oh, I am terribly sorry to hear about that." You, in turn, may become defensive and feel compelled to offer an explanation of the circumstances surrounding the divorce. You're not even sure what you yourself consider an appropriate response. If someone said, "Hmmm, that's very interesting. How did that all come about?" you would probably be equally surprised and wonder why this news was taken so matter of factly.

Obviously, your child should be the first to know about the decision to divorce. I think it is also important for you to let other people know about the divorce as soon as possible. Some people simply let a few of their friends and relatives know and rely on them to spread the information, but this can be dangerous because you cannot know exactly what version of the story has been passed around, and what distortions of the facts have occurred.

Informing others may not be pleasant, but it is a necessary process and, if it is done properly, it will minimize your future problems. Because so many listeners are going to be awkward in their responses, curious about the details and yet reluctant to ask, it is wise to present more than simply the news of your decision to divorce. How much information you offer is a personal matter. I do not think you should go into great detail, nor should you elaborate upon your feelings. The reason for informing others is to help them adjust to your new status so that your relationship with them can continue to be meaningful. If you avoid informing the people who are involved in your everyday life you may find that they feel awkward toward you because you did not tell them directly, and they may even avoid you.

They're not sure you wanted them to know in the first place, and they don't want to betray their source.

The importance of informing others extends to professional contacts. It is important for your doctors to know about your changed circumstances, since divorce can have a marked effect on your health. It is a substantial stress in your life and can account for changes in your physical state. Loss of appetite, loss of weight, a rise in blood pressure, lack of energy, and other physical symptoms can have different meanings to your doctor if he or she knows you are undergoing, or have just gone through, a divorce. Your doctors can also revise their files, and make sure they do not transmit information concerning your health to your former spouse or a member of his or her family.

Children usually have routine medical examinations as part of school requirements. Their doctors should also be informed of the change in family structure as a matter of course, so that the child's health can be viewed in the context of this change. Generally speaking, doctors try to avoid taking sides in a divorce, and you should not place them in a position where they are pressured to do so. Your children's doctor is in a particularly difficult position as he tries to keep open lines of communication with you and your child. These lines of communication can be altered in subtle ways, possibly affecting the efforts to maintain continuity in your child's life.

It is also important to inform teachers and the parents of your child's friends. The information you give should be informative, but not overly detailed. Try to relate the facts as simply as you can. It is disconcerting to be told, "I am glad you told me about the divorce, but please, I don't want to get involved with all the details." Hard as it may be, you might just as well accept the fact that no one is as interested in your divorce as you are. I have often observed that people going through divorce who persist in burdening others with details begin to find their friends and relatives less and less accessible.

As tempting as it is, try not to drag your friends, relatives, and your children's teachers into the awkward situation of having to concede, based on your story, that you are completely correct and your spouse is totally at fault. Some parents deal with a divorce by "choosing up sides." It is as if they are conducting a popularity contest and their strength or credibility lies in the total number of people they can win over to their side. A child is faced with an extremely difficult situation when he finds that friends and relatives of the family have lined up as allies of one parent and enemies of the other. It intensifies the child's difficulties in dealing with other people.

Frequently it's awkward for your mutual friends to relate to you when you are going through a divorce. They may feel pulled in one direction or the other, and find it impossible to continue seeing you both. They may see one and give up the other; and sometimes they find it easier to give up both. At this particular time you need all the emotional support you can get, but you must face the possibility that some of your friends will drift away from you.

Most of your friends who are relatively stable and content with their own lives will show compassion and sympathy, but even they will *not* want to get deeply involved with your problems and your feelings. You will find, however, that there are other friends and relatives who not only seem to show a great deal of sympathy and concern, but may even revel in your misery. I agree that this is a reverse kind of satisfaction; for in a sense they are saying to themselves, consciously or unconsciously, "I am glad it is you and not me who is suffering." As strange as it may seem, unhappily married friends or those who are aware of the weaknesses in their own marital situations are precisely those who are likely to come forth and give you a great deal of advice and become deeply involved with you and your problems. Be careful. These people may be trying to solve their own problems by telling you what they should be telling themselves. They speak like experts, with great authority. You, in your exhausted and highly vulnerable state, in need of all the support and assurance you can get, can fall prey to these people who seem to have your best interests at heart, but whose reactions and counsel are actually destructive.

For this reason it is important to have professional help to assist you in mapping out your course of action. Don't hesitate to consult professionals if you are in the dark or overwhelmed. Since you will have to make many important decisions concerning your life and your children's, get the best advice possible. The professionals you may find helpful are lawyers, psychiatrists, psychologists, and social workers, as well as educators, financial advisers, and others who are expert in particular fields. Your friends may mean well but they can rarely offer the same skills and experience as experts. You owe it to yourself to get the best help possible.

No matter how important your friends and relatives are to you at this time, the most critical issue in a divorce is how you deal with the other parent. Since most divorces take place in an atmosphere of hostility, there is a great temptation to sustain this hostility through all the important decisions to be taken about your future and your children's future. Remember, divorce is a great stress that challenges every control you have. Even when you use all the resources you have available, you are still going to reel under the emotional upheaval. No matter how stable and well adjusted you think you are, you will find yourself hard-pressed to retain your self-control. Whatever strengths you have, you will need. Whatever weaknesses you have will be accentuated.

Many people undergoing divorce experience severe emotional reactions that appear to effect a personality change. They can become so immobilized that their ability to make decisions and to think problems through is seriously impaired, or they may turn into raging despots, despite their previously tranquil nature. This sounds like terribly strong language, but it is actually descriptive of what I have seen happen to many people going through divorce. Others still, who have very trusting natures, are overcome with suspiciousness and paranoid feelings. In general these character changes are transitory and eventually subside, if for no other reason than from sheer exhaustion.

It is important to realize the implications of the turmoil I have been describing, not only for yourself but also for the other parent. You will be more inclined to interpret the intense reactions of your spouse largely as responses to the stress of the situation. Even with this awareness, the buildup of tension is so great at times, and your need to ventilate your feelings so intense, that you may often act against your better judgment.

There is little control over a wife's feelings of anger and intense hurt when a divorce is precipitated by a husband who has just fallen in love with the seductive new office secretary twenty years younger than she is. An equally explosive situation exists when a wife reveals to her husband that she wants to divorce him because for the past three years she has been having an affair with his closest friend. The intensity of these feelings is so overwhelming, and the frustration of the circumstances so immobilizing, that you can easily be tempted to lash out and hurt in whatever way you can. You are likely to strike out simply to preserve whatever integrity you still have in the face of your uncertainty and powerlessness. If this happens, your child can easily become a weapon in the battle when the time comes to divide the property and decide where the child will live. You can strike back at your spouse, but you shouldn't. Your child will be the one to suffer, not the secretary twenty years younger than you.

The more acrimonious the divorce, the more easily the children will be caught in the crossfire. I do not mean to imply that the intensity of feeling between the parents is the key factor in determining the negative impact of divorce on the child, because it is not. The point I want to emphasize is that the vulnerability of the child is higher when the tempers are hotter.

Olivia is an example of one of my patients caught in the crossfire of the ongoing battle her mother was waging. Olivia's mother was deeply distraught at her impending divorce. Even though she initiated it, she felt justified in making her husband's life as miserable as she could. She seemed compelled to hurt him in every way possible, and wasn't the least bit inhibited about doing it in front of Olivia. Olivia loved her father and constantly defended him, but her mother kept saying, "He's mean and deserves this."

Olivia told me of one incident which left an indelible trace on her memory. Her father was having his coffee in the morning and received a phone call. While he was speaking on the phone, her mother deliberately took his cup and poured the coffee in the sink. He took it in stride and didn't react, knowing it would only cause more turmoil and make Olivia a weapon in the situation, but Olivia screamed in accusation at her mother. She became so distraught she required psychological help.

In her sessions with me, Olivia described another episode in which her mother took a pair of scissors and cut the legs off the trousers of her father's favorite suit. No matter how hard I tried to explain to Olivia that her mother was unhappy and angry, she still protested that what her mother did was wrong. I had to agree with her, and unfortunately she was never able to forgive her mother for what she had done.

I do feel strongly that even though you should not fight outwardly with your spouse during the divorce process, you do not need to be a "doormat" or allow yourself to be taken advantage of during this time. Some people feel they have to capitulate to their spouse's wishes or they will be viewed as uncooperative. It is not only possible but necessary to work problems out without either selling yourself short or taking a stubborn and unyielding position. It does not help to yield on issues simply to make the point that you are "giving" or "cooperative." Holding your own and protecting your integrity is appropriate. Yielding to some degree is a sign of a healthy willingness to compromise, but giving in on issues that weaken your self-esteem can be viewed as allowing yourself to be a doormat.

While I support cooperative attitudes between parents, I am not suggesting that you adopt a superficial "lovey-dovey" stance in doing so. This too can be confusing to a child. After all, if you get along so well and are excessively considerate toward each other, your child is likely to wonder why you are getting divorced in the first place. You simply intensify your child's ambivalent feelings of love and anger that occur simultaneously.

Any efforts on your part to preserve your child's love for you and for the other parent will be rewarding for everyone involved. Even if your child has accepted the divorce intellectually as the best possible resolution of your marital problem, at the most primitive level of his feelings he still wishes everything were perfect, that you and your spouse loved each other, that there were no family tensions, financial problems, or obstacles to your living happily ever after as a family.

Even though you and your spouse are no longer a team, you still have your children and their needs to deal with. Although it is best to have two parents involved in the rearing of children, the nature of divorce makes this extremely difficult. It is hoped that the parent who is primarily responsible for the child's welfare and education can have sufficiently adequate communication with the other parent to be able to freely transmit information concerning the child's health and progress in school. Some parents embittered by the divorce will nevertheless insist on attending teachers' conferences with their former spouse. These meetings often turn into knock-down-drag-out arguments. As a result, many schools now arrange conferences with each parent separately; and in some instances, schools will arrange conferences only with the custodial spouse.

It is amazing to see how many people consciously or unconsciously attempt to maintain a relationship with the divorced spouse through legal machinations or willful refusal to work out the details for forming a life apart. In fact, some people make the divorce a *cause célèbre*. It becomes their primary activity, their focus of conversation, and the motivating force behind all their actions and decisions. A persisting and overpowering feeling of vindictiveness toward an ex-spouse delays attempts to build a new life for oneself.

Men and women who engage in prolonged anger or other negative expressions may subconsciously be clinging to the partner they are divorcing. Paradoxical as it may seem, marriages can be held together over a long period of time through mutual anger, vindictiveness, or hate. Divorced couples who continue their relationship through these negative and destructive processes are not emotionally divorced.

Any matter involving continued responsibility to each other or requiring a cooperative effort is a potential battleground. When one spouse remains dependent on the other, emotionally or otherwise, there can be no successful resolution of the divorce. One of the key areas that causes conflict and mutual resentment is the issue of financial dependency. It places one person in the position of being dependent upon the other after the deterioration of a relationship, and the latter to have to pay for the dependency of the former. Moreover, feelings of dependency cause conflict. There is resentment in being dependent and at the same time an opportunity to hurt the ex-spouse through the "penalty" of large support payments. Continued economic dependency following divorce can prevent the dependent spouse from developing resources for self-sufficiency. It also perpetuates a relationship when none is desired, and in a way that encourages increasingly greater resentment.

If one person in the family has been the primary source of economic support, in all likelihood that person now has to maintain two households with the same amount of money that had previously been used to maintain one. The alternative is to put in more time working to earn more money. Although working longer may ease the economic burden, it obviously decreases the time available for other purposes. There is no escaping the reality of the fact that financial matters play an important role in divorce and its outcome. Bluntly put, some people do not have sufficient resources to support two households after divorce in the manner to which each was accustomed. Under these circumstances, divorce requires major changes in life style; and at best, this is difficult.

Clearly, prolonging the battle simply extends the length of the divorce process and ironically keeps both partners involved emotionally simply because of the unresolved anger and dependency. The true sign of divorce psychologically and emotionally, is to have achieved an attitude of relative indifference toward your former spouse rather than to continue a relationship based on negative feelings.

The following questions and responses reflect a sample of those that have arisen in my professional consultations with people going through divorce.

The turmoil of my divorce has finally gotten to me. I vacillate between feeling that everyone is out to get me and feeling that I will trust anybody who offers a friendly word of advice. At times I feel as if I am on the verge of a nervous breakdown because I can't make any decisions by myself. My closest friend tells me the only ones who win in divorces are the lawyers—and for that reason I should do *anything* to get it over with quickly even if I have to give in on some disputed points. I just don't know. Whose advice should I take?"

It's always hard to make decisions when you are under great stress and uncertain about which direction to take. The desire to get all the decisions over with as quickly as possible is understandable. During your distress you feel as if anything is worth the price simply to end the uncertainty. You should move matters along quickly but not foolishly. I don't believe you should make *any* concessions simply to shorten the period of turmoil; you'll have a long time to live with the decisions you made in haste. Once the terms of the divorce are finalized it's quite common for people to regret many of the concessions they made. When that time comes you will feel "taken advantage of" and the victim of poor advice.

It's easy to say "the only ones who win in divorces are the

lawyers." Although this may sometimes be true, it's hardly the general rule. Legal costs are indeed high, but the services of any skilled professional are costly. This kind of remark is likely to create greater anxiety for you and cause you to doubt the lawyer in whom you've invested your trust, making it difficult to work constructively. If you have mixed feelings about your lawyer, as many people do, a remark like this can lead you to find excessive fault with him and cause you to bounce from lawyer to lawyer.

I don't mean to imply that any advice from a friend is bad. Friends can be very helpful and supportive; but make sure you don't allow other people's prejudices to drive you toward binding decisions you will regret for a long time to come.

"My husband refuses to move out of the house even though we are in the midst of divorce proceedings. We're not sure yet how things will work out, but in the meantime I'm afraid the tension will be too much for our children. Isn't it best for one parent to move out and leave the children with the other parent?"

Many people think that the problems children develop after the parents announce their decision to divorce result from the tension surrounding the divorce. This leads them to believe that once the decision to divorce has been made, one parent should move out as quickly as possible, to minimize further tensions. Actually, it is not always advisable for a parent to move out immediately; a child can easily feel abandoned by the parent who has moved out, especially during this period of extreme emotional stress. To have one parent automatically move out at the time of the decision to divorce is as thought-less a procedure as the idea that two unhappy people should remain together simply for the sake of the children.

"I am terribly bothered by the fact that my ex-husband refuses to communicate with me directly. I have tried on a number of occasions but only get nasty or sarcastic responses. He constantly refers me to his lawyer and uses the children during their weekly visits as the intermediary for any communication he wants to make with me. Doesn't it put a great deal of pressure on a child to be placed in the position of spokesperson for a father who is so angry and vindictive that he won't communicate with me on matters that concern his children directly?''

Yes, it is unfair to a child to be placed in that position. Unfortunately, however, there is no way you can force your former husband to communicate with you directly if he does not want to. If your children are stable and happy and have a good relationship with you, I am sure they will understand the position you are in. Don't hesitate to explain to them that you would much prefer to speak directly with their father rather than have him transmit messages through them, but that unfortunately he is still angry with you and feels he can't talk to you. Avoid allowing your children to take on the same role for you. It might be better if you established some means of communication through your own lawyer.

Obviously, it would be to everyone's advantage if the communication between two former spouses were to be maintained on a reasonable basis. Psychologically speaking, when anger persists over a period of time it reflects some unresolved emotional tie with the ex-spouse. Your husband's intense anger in some way indicates feelings he still has for you, negative though they are. Only when all these emotions are neutralized and there is a feeling of relative indifference are a couple truly divorced in an emotional sense. Then and only then does full communication become possible, especially on matters concerning children. You can only hope that this will eventually happen in your case.

"I have always been very close to my cousin and his wife. They are about to get divorced and each has asked me to take part in what looks to be a long-drawn-out court battle. I can't tell you how upset I am, and frankly I don't know how to handle this or what to tell them."

You are indeed in a difficult position. Unfortunately, a divorce involves many more people than the two partners in a marriage. I have seen many close families torn apart by a divorce; I know of brothers and sisters who have become estranged because of circumstances surrounding a divorce. The potential for disruption is far-reaching.

I think it's best for you to be frank and open with both your cousin and his wife. Let them each know how close you feel to each of them and how much you would like to maintain a positive relationship with both of them after the divorce. Point out that it will be impossible for you to do this if you are drawn to one side or the other. As hard as it will be to maintain a position of neutrality or detachment in the situation, if you truly believe that you do not favor one partner's position over the other's, this should be your goal. If you feel strongly toward one partner, however, you may feel obligated to offer support to him or her in the legal entanglement. If this is the case and you do get drawn into the legal battle, prepare yourself for the fact that your relationship with the other partner will most likely suffer irreparable damage.

Relatives are frequently brought into divorce proceedings and, as a general rule, support *blood* lines. When a blood relative of one party in the divorce offers testimony in support of the other party, it can be very damaging, both legally and psychologically. For example, if you were to testify for your cousin's wife rather than your cousin, it would weigh heavily against your cousin since you would be going against tradition by "betraying" a blood relative.

It sounds to me as if you want to avoid taking sides in order to preserve your relationship with both your cousin and his wife. Although I sympathize with this intention, you should realize that even if you make this clear to them, each may temporarily see your choice as beneficial to the adversary spouse and feel annoyed or even angry with you. Nevertheless, your neutrality will put you in a better position to maintain or revive your relationship with each of them at some future point. Once you have taken a position for one side and against the other it is extremely difficult, if not impossible, to eliminate the resentment this can cause.

"My husband is a despicable beast and has done cruel things to me. I want my children to know all about this. I resent the children expressing affection for their father and feel they are going to suffer in the long run if they fail to see what he is *really* like. I know I'm very upset now—I daydream about terrible things happening to him and I fantasize how I can get back at him for all the hurt he's caused me. I also dream of falling in love with a wonderful man who loves me and makes me forget all the pain I've suffered with this awful beast I'm still married to.

"Do you think I'm wrong to let my children know what their father is really like? Everyone says I'm being foolish and that if I tell my children it will hurt them rather than help them. Is this true?"

It is important for you to sort out those problems which are yours and those problems which you share with your children. The fact that you are hurt by what your husband has done does not justify burdening your children with problems they cannot deal with effectively. Your children need your help with *their* own problems and concerns, and they will suffer if they concentrate on your emotions rather than on their own. Furthermore, no one benefits in the end. You can be sure that your children will sort out their feelings for each of you and will appreciate you more for not having burdened them with your problems—maybe not immediately, but certainly in the end.

Remember, your role as a parent is to help your children mobilize their own resources in any of life's crises—and divorce is no exception. In fact, they need your help more at this time because they need to work out any ambivalent feelings they may have toward their parents, and ways in which they can continue to love each of them in spite of the parents' changed feelings for each other.

Clearly, if both parents are cooperative, notwithstanding occasional irritations or sarcastic remarks, they can work out the details of a divorce while preserving in the eyes and hearts of their children an image of strength as well as tenderness. I am *not* suggesting that you should demand respect from children toward a parent who is cruel, exploitative, or rejecting. All I suggest is that you take precautions not to demean the character of their father or reject a child for having positive feelings for him.

As intense as your feelings may become with the build-up of frustration and your inability to defuse your anger, you will feel closer to your children and they will feel more protected by you if you resolve the marital situation without physical abuse or degrading comments about your husband. When tempers flare and anger is expressed, these emotions can be directed at issues rather than at the integrity of your husband. Your behavior can serve as a model to your children for dealing with conflict situations as well as relationships that change over time.

I fully sympathize with your position during this difficult time. Your existence is fragmented and you crave structure. I think fantasies not only provide relief, but also help you envision a new life for yourself. If you're going to fantasize, you might as well fantasize the ultimate in happiness. While dreams may not be based on reality, they are nonetheless satisfaction.

Prepare yourself for an active fantasy life during this tough period of conflict and transition. In fact, fantasy can serve you well. Your hostility and vengeful feelings can better be expressed in fantasy than in reality.

"I am particularly concerned with the problems a parent faces when he or she is the one who no longer wants to continue in a marriage. In my case, I have two children, one eleven and the other fourteen, who have always been much closer to their father than to me. I am the one who wants out of the marriage; my husband doesn't. The children are aware of this. What special problems can I anticipate for myself and for my children?"

For very obvious reasons your children will see you as the one who is breaking up the family. Whether or not they understand the reasons behind your decision, they are sure to resent you for the divorce. In circumstances like yours in which the children feel closest to the parent who does not initiate the divorce, the relationship frequently becomes even closer. In some ways a situation such as yours may put less of an emotional burden on the children, because they are less inclined to feel that they have caused the divorce.

I am assuming from your question that your children would prefer to live with their father. If this is not the case, or if they are forced to live with you, I am certain you will have a great many difficulties dealing with their resentment for the disruption in their lives. If their wishes are granted as to which parent they prefer to live with, and if you avoid pulling them into any problem the divorce creates for you, I believe you will be able to maintain a good relationship with your children once the turmoil of the divorce is over. In time, I am sure you will be able to explain your reasons for wanting the divorce.

Financial considerations frequently complicate an already difficult emotional situation. If the parent who initiates the divorce is the one who has the greater earning ability, the children may feel a threat to the life style to which they have been accustomed, and may therefore experience a greater resentment toward that parent. For example, the father may initiate a divorce and leave a wife who has few if any resources for earning an adequate income to care for the children. In this case the children would feel a greater responsibility for, and more sympathy toward, the parent who did not initiate the divorce, and the father who initiated the action would be the focus of greater resentment. Frequently, the parent who initiates the divorce feels more intense guilt about the family disruption, and the other parent feels greater self-pity and self-righteousness. Under these circumstances intense guilt can lead to overcompensation through indulging the children, or the parent can feel so overwhelmed by guilt that he or she finds it hard to face the children and has increasingly less contact with them.

Obviously, if the remaining parent has stability—and I am talking of both emotional and economic stability—the family unit will suffer less disruption and have more resources available for stabilizing itself without a substantial drain on the emotions of the children.

CHAPTER 6

WHO SHALL
HAVE CUSTODY?

I THINK EACH parent should confront the difficult question, "Do I *really* want custody of my children?"

While the question is tough, the answer may be even tougher, for it is frequently painful to arrive at an honest answer. I know many parents who have children secretly wish that they had never had them in the first place. It is very hard to admit this to themselves, or to anyone. I am convinced as well that many people who divorce do not want the burden of having their children. Nevertheless, they may struggle to get custody simply because of the social image involved. This is particularly true of women, and we live in a society where mothers have traditionally been awarded custody of the children unless proven unfit or unless they relinquished custody willingly. In the latter case, society looks upon the mother as abandoning her children.

It is unfair for women to bear the burden of this stigma, particularly if they know the father would like custody and is competent to meet the needs of the children. If a parent does not sincerely want custody of the children, having them is burdensome and unpleasant, and these feelings are naturally reflected in the attitudes that parent expresses toward the children.

In other words, if you do not want custody, do not try to get it. If you are truly concerned with your children's best interests, you will ignore any criticism that you are abandoning them. If you feel that your spouse is indeed a better parent, or if you feel you need a life of your own and that parental responsibility is too great a burden, do not hesitate to relinquish custody—provided this meets with the approval of your children and the acceptance of your spouse.

If you relinquish custody of your children, this does not necessarily mean you are unfit as a parent. Your basic concerns should be (a) how do you really feel about your children; (b) who is truly the better parent psychologically; and (c) what are your children's wishes in regard to living arrangements. These concerns must be your primary consideration in arranging custody. In my experience, those parents who respected their children's wishes and let go had a far better relationship for a longer time than those parents who automatically followed the prescribed social pattern regardless of the children's wishes.

I do not believe that mothers or fathers should be given custody of a child based upon their gender. This statement cannot be overemphasized. The assumption of the biological or psychological superiority of one parent is unfair to the other parent, and above all, unfair to their children.

When both parents want custody and each feels equally competent to handle the needs of children, the situation requires careful adjudication and serious evaluation of the capability of each parent to be sole custodian of the children. What are the qualities one should look for?

While it is very difficult to list specific elements that are all-inclusive and easily interpreted and measured, there are some general qualities I consider important in judging a parent's capacity to provide emotional security for a child. When the child is either too young to choose or reluctant to do so, the judge or professional should attempt to look for the following qualities in a parents' attitudes and feelings toward the child: a deep love and affection, expressed with consistency; a genuine acceptance of the child; and an involvement in the child's life that nurtures emotional growth.

More and more instances have come to my attention where neither parent truly wants custody of the children. This is indeed tragic. The child's worst fears of being abandoned have come true. The solution to this problem requires careful evaluation of the capability and desire of relatives or friends for taking custody of the child. Ideally this situation could be prevented if more people were aware of the commitment and responsibility of parenthood before having children.

I believe it imperative that universal parenthood education be provided starting in elementary school. We need to impress upon our youth the importance of making a commitment to the serious responsibilities of becoming a parent. The course would also discuss the alternative of *not* becoming a parent at all if both the man and woman do not want to accept the primary responsibility of caring for the children. In this way both men and women would be equally prepared and knowledgeable and could share parenthood more equally. In the case of divorce, each would be on equal ground when it came to parental competence.

Historically, the question "Who will get custody of the children?" was hardly ever asked. Custody was determined by a seemingly immutable judicial procedure based upon precedent rather than careful scrutiny of the facts. The unfounded psychological notion that mothers are innately better equipped for being parents lent support to the rigidity of judicial thinking. Getting divorced was synonymous with "Mother will get the children and Father will pay for their care." Courts did not allow children the possibility of having their father as their legal custodian unless the mother was proven totally unfit. I am not using the term "totally" lightly. Judges routinely awarded children to mothers even with clear evidence of the mother's misconduct, emotional instability, alcoholism, or neglect. There was even a case where the mother and her male friends involved the children in pornographic acts, documented with photographs, and even this evidence was not considered by the court sufficiently damaging to deny custody to the mother.

As extreme as this example is, it exemplifies the tragic nature of certain presumptions that prevailed in deciding custody cases. Not only were fathers forced to gather destructive information about the mother, but they would almost always fail in their attempt to gain custody because of the presumption that the mother was innately the better parent. The child was clearly deprived of his constitutional right to due process of law. Fathers were defeated before they began; for this reason many fathers chose not to attempt to gain custody, even when they were demonstrably better equipped to raise their children. Few lawyers were willing to offer any optimism for appealing to the court for a fair judgment of a father's competence as a parent. This view is not simply conjecture on my part; it is based on solid personal experience. A father could be effectively forced to abandon his children and sit by helplessly even if the children would sustain psychological or physical neglect if awarded to the mother.

The laws of most states stipulate that the best interests of the child should be given prime consideration, and many states also mandate that both parents have equal rights to custody of the children. But what is so frustrating is that neither the best-interest concept nor the equal-access concept has been practiced. The legal injustice is bad enough; the psychological injustice and the potential damage it can create in the life of a child are immeasurable.

A major step in the right direction took place with the passage of a resolution by the American Psychological Association's Council of Representatives. The resolution reads:

> Be it resolved that the Council of Representatives recognizes officially and makes suitable promulgation of the fact that it is scientifically and psychologically baseless as well as in violation of human rights to discriminate against men because of their sex in assignment of children's custody, in adoption, in the staffing of child-care services, in personnel practices providing for parental leave in relation to childbirth and emergencies involving children, and in similar laws and practices. Further, it is recommended that suitable promulgation of the resolution (with the paragraphs providing the rationale) include specific mailing to the Chief Justice of the United States Supreme Court in his capacity as the chief administrative officer of the Federal court system, to the presiding judges of the various state court systems, to the Attorney General of the United States, and to the Attorneys General of the states.

Thus has the most highly respected body of psychologists in the country taken a stand on the legal rights of fathers. The resolution could be used as expert testimony in court on this most important issue.

"Equal access" and "best interests" are two basically fair concepts. If interpreted properly, they mean that in deciding custody the judge would determine which parent would be *better* able to meet the physical and emotional needs of the child. It is a fact of life that not all people are equally good at all things, and parenthood is no exception. We should *not* look down upon people who may, perhaps, be less nurturant, or less effective in meeting the needs of their children, any more than we should look down upon someone who is a good cook, but not as good as his or her spouse.

It is absolutely essential that we abandon the negative approach—proving unfitness—and adopt the positive approach of determining who is better able to meet the needs of a child. In this way the question of custody could be decided on the basis of the issues in question, without bias against one gender or the other, without defaming the character of one parent or the other, and without creating the stigma that a person is unfit if his or her spouse is considered better at being a parent.

Children also suffer in the turmoil of divorce when they are used as hostages, particularly in acrimonious divorces. Unfortunately there are few legal procedures for protecting a child from being used in this way. Many people profess to respect a child's feelings, yet in a divorce use their children as hostages to gain material benefits or psychological advantages. Clearly, placing a child in this position is an indignity, and can not only cause undue hardship for the child but can also undermine his sense of self-importance. Moreover, if the child sees a human being manipulate another human being without any compassion whatsoever, it could set a model for the child himself to use human beings in a manipulative way.

In my work with parents and children I have repeatedly seen one parent interfere with a child's visit to the other parent simply because a certain payment was not made or the child support was late; in revenge, the child is forbidden to go to his other parent. Very often the revenge backfires; the child deeply resents the parent who has sabotaged a cherished relationship in order to gain certain financial ends. More frequently than I care to relate, I have seen children offered by one parent to the other in return for a better property settlement.

Visitation arrangements are every bit as important an issue for your child's welfare as the original custody decision. I recommend the same legal recognition for children in matters concerning visitation as in custody arrangements. All too often, visitation is set up arbitrarily and can be manipulated by a vengeful parent later on. Parents frequently speak of *"my* weekend" or *"my* visitation." Actually, it is the child's weekend and the child's visitation. Here again, we have a situation where adults are inclined to "own" a child's life, or treat a child like a prisoner. To force visitation against his or her wishes increases resentment.

One eight-year-old boy named David began to show intense anger and picked on younger children. His father was concerned with the reports his teacher was sending home, and brought David to me to help get to the bottom of the boy's anger and aggressiveness. His parents were divorced, and David didn't seem to object to the custody arrangements. In fact, he said, most things were much better now that the divorce was over, but he was very unhappy because he couldn't do many things his friends could do. For example, he couldn't spend a weekend at a friend's country home because his mother insisted it was *her* weekend and wouldn't let him go. As he talked about his mother's unfairness, his anger mounted. When Christmas and spring vacation came around he couldn't go away on holiday trips either, because his time had to be equally divided between his parents.

David even tried to trade off visitation days so he could have a life of his own; he offered to pay his mother back in days if she would let him go on trips or spend time with his friends during his visitation days with her. She held fast to her "rights" on this matter, but David kept asking, "What about *my* rights?" He was understandably angry and felt mistreated both by this legal judgment and his mother's rigid adherence to it. His mother's refusal to budge on the matter caused him great anguish: "She doesn't care about me or my feelings. She doesn't respect me, she's only interested in herself."

David wanted to love and respect his mother but found it impossible to do so because of her unreasonable position. Yet if the divorce agreement had allowed for flexibility or periodic reevaluation of the visitation arrangements, David and his mother would have been able to maintain a more harmonious relationship and his frustration would not have built to the point where he showed disturbed behavior.

There are many examples of parents who are able to deal with issues constructively in spite of their anger toward one another. Twelve-year-old Mark had a problem with his visitation days. He wanted to earn money to buy a motorbike, which meant doing odd jobs after school and on weekends. Although he wanted to visit his father during the court-arranged visitation time on Saturday and Sunday, he realized he couldn't visit and hold a job at the same time. His mother and father were responsive to his needs and feelings, and adapted his visits so as not to interfere with his emerging desire to work and take on responsibility. Both parents were very cooperative in working out visitation so that Mark could continue to do the things he wanted without compromising his desire to be with each parent. Their cooperation contributed to Mark's feeling that each of his parents loved him and cared about his wishes.

Mark realized that his parents no longer loved one another and was grateful that their reasonable behavior toward his problems allowed him to love them both without guilt or discomfort. They respected his feelings in spite of their own conflict.

At a time when there is a growing effort to have parents share child-rearing commitments during marriage, many people have given consideration to joint custody in an attempt to preserve equal responsibility and prevent the exclusion of one parent from full participation in the decisions affecting the child's future.

In some circumstances joint custody might work effectively, but it must be given careful consideration as an alternative to single-parent custody. Realistically speaking, it would not work in those cases where parents are still at war with each other. When each parent has equal responsibility for a child's well-being, that child is clearly vulnerable to becoming the focus of conflict.

Although joint custody does turn into a battle in many instances, it can work for parents who have come to terms with their own problems and with their relationship to one another. It can be an attractive option for judges and lawyers, since it may make their job easier.

However, I cannot support the concept of joint custody on that basis alone. It is important to realize that "joint custody" may simply be a euphemism, a solution that is dictated more by efforts to save the integrity of both parents than to protect the interests of the child. In essence it implies that neither parent is giving up "ownership" of the child, but instead that both parents are equally adequate in meeting the needs of the child. However, in practice, the parent with whom the child lives is the one who generally makes the decisions and has responsibility for the child.

If joint custody is arranged so that each parent has equal time with the children, obviously the responsibility for decisions shifts with the living arrangements unless there is an alternative agreement concerning decisions. As you can see, joint custody requires the utmost cooperation between the parents, a minimum of animosity, and the best possible communication process. In most divorces, these circumstances hardly prevail. Moreover, I have to raise the question whether it is truly best for a child to be placed in a situation in which he or she can so easily manipulate the parents by playing off one against the other.

The child in a situation of joint custody is not at all unlike an employee who has two bosses, each with equal voice. Not only can the employee be victimized by any competitiveness or hostility between the two bosses, but he is also in a position to generate friction between them. Joint custody in my opinion is not a panacea, but one option to be considered in making judgments concerning custody. If it is tried, every effort should be made to protect the children from getting caught in the crossfire between the parents.

Clearly, the matter of child custody is a crucial one, if not the most crucial, when a marriage comes to an end. So much of a child's later life will be shaped by it that parents should give the utmost care and consideration to its resolution. If we respect a child as a thinking and feeling person who is sensitive to what is happening and give him a role in arranging his life after the divorce, he can be stronger for having done so. He will learn to view family problems as solvable without loss of self-esteem, and above all, will be respectful of his parents for their sincere interest in his feelings even though they have grown apart over the years of their marriage.

The following are some of the questions and responses that have arisen in my professional consultations on matters concerning custody.

"In attempting to evaluate psychological competence in a parent, what do you look for? It's such a subjective matter and is determined by the values, prejudices, and views of the person making such a judgment. I realize you can't be very specific, but with your training and experience you must have some idea what judges, lawyers, and other professionals should look for."

Basically, competence in parenting means being able to meet your child's needs. From the behavioral point of view, there are six qualities, discussed below, that I consider most important in evaluating parental competence.

Acceptance. A child should feel you accept her unconditionally. Whatever she may do that you dislike, she should feel accepted by you—that she belongs no matter how disobedient she may be.

Affection. Children need to feel your warmth and love. They need to have that occasional hug, kiss, or pat on the back that represents your sincere feelings. The gesture without sincere feelings will never fool a child into believing it sincere. Loving the child and demonstrating it one moment and rejecting him and showing anger the next moment, without any rational basis, leaves a child anxious and fearful of losing your love. I am not suggesting that you never show annoyance or anger; I am simply pointing out that affection should be consistent.

Approval. It is essential that a parent express approval of a child's behavior, accomplishments, and feelings. As ironic as it might sound, expressing approval includes expressing disapproval as well. You have to let your child know how you feel, and he must sense your approval or disapproval of the things he does. This is in direct contrast to those parents who show no reaction whatsoever, unless their child gets into trouble. Unfortunately, many parents respond to their children only when they do things wrong, and pay attention only to their weaknesses, not to their accomplishments. After being treated this way, a child tends to give up seeking approval, and may show low motivation for learning. It also encourages him to gain parental recognition through failures, rather than successes.

Protection. When I speak of protection, I mean showing your child that you care about his safety. There are some parents who believe children have to learn everything for themselves. They might sit by and watch as a child climbs a high fence, feeling that "if he falls he will learn his lesson," despite the fact that he might also fracture his skull. I do not mean to suggest that you keep your child from climbing, but that you stand by and assist him in a protective way, explaining what the consequences would be if he were to lose his footing. (Not allowing him to climb in the first place would be overprotective.)

Years ago, efforts were made to prevent children from being exposed to psychological traumas in the same way that they were protected from physical hazards. I believe traumatic events are not necessarily detrimental to a child; it is the child's inability to cope with them that is. A child learns to cope with traumatic experiences by being exposed to them and by having the assistance of parents in developing those resources needed to deal with them, both at the present time and as a model for problems that will inevitably arise later in life. A person going on a fishing trip in an unknown area is wise to take on a guide. That means going with someone who knows the area and can help you to achieve your goal more readily. That guide does not fish for you—he simply gives you the assistance necessary to get to the point where you yourself achieve that goal.

Guidance. This quality overlaps somewhat with protection. Parents must give children options and a sense of freedom. But they must define the limits of that freedom, both to help the children achieve success and, at the same time, to protect them from possible harm. Without guidance, a child can not only get lost and wander aimlessly, but can also become permanently frustrated and fear making any choices.

Discipline. Discipline refers to rules and regulations that define what is acceptable and unacceptable behavior. Unfortunately, it is frequently confused with punishment. Punishment is essentially the "price" you pay for violating a rule. In my way of thinking, discipline is an extension of a parent's love for a child. The parent who sets no limits is offering no protection, no guidance, and no means of showing approval or disapproval.

As you can see, while discipline is somewhat different from the other five qualities, it incorporates them all. Children who have no limits set for them frequently feel that no one cares about them. You must apply the rules and regulations consistently, and this includes threats and promises as well. They not only need discipline, but they actually enjoy it. Children love to play games; with little or no equipment they create their own games which, in essence, are sets of rules that require conformity as well as challenge.

The judgments of any professional evaluating these six qualities will of course be subjective, and require trained skills and sensitivity based on experience. But this is not necessarily a weakness. For the most part, judgments made in court are subjective, which doesn't necessarily make them invalid. While checklists or rating scales can be developed to evaluate these qualities in a way that leads to a more objective analysis, a great deal can be lost in reducing human qualities to a checklist.

"I can understand the value of letting a child's wishes be a determining factor in deciding which parent gets custody. However, I frankly don't believe it's possible to get the truth from a child about whom he truly wants to live with, since children are easily swayed by things they want. No one can tell me that a child whose lifelong ambition has been to own a red two-wheeler bicycle could not be enticed to say 'I want to live with my father' if the father promised him the bike if he would agree to come with him. Isn't there a more objective way of evaluating a child's wishes than to ask him?"

A child, or anyone else for that matter, *can* be enticed to make a decision in a given direction with the help of many lures. But I still believe that you can get the truth from a child about his wishes and at the same time discern the reasons behind his choice. Deciding whom a child wants to live with is more complicated a procedure than simply asking him which parent he chooses. It requires an in-depth discussion about his life and interests with a professional who can establish a good rapport with him and assure a high degree of confidentiality.

There are no concrete techniques that I can advise, since the matter is a very subjective one. Yet the fact that the interpretation of a child's responses is subjective in nature does not detract from its value. Oftentimes reducing something to an objective, statistical approach robs it of its human quality. I would agree that it would be difficult to base a decision solely on what a child tells one or the other of his parents, since most children would like to tell their parents what they would like to hear. This is a form of ingratiation that serves to maintain close feelings between the parent and the child. Similarly, it would be very hard for a child to tell one parent that he prefers to live with the other parent. A child in that position would be inclined to answer such a direct question with "I don't know."

As difficult as it is to establish the validity of a child's choice, it is still an important question to pursue, while making it clear that his preferring to live with one parent does not mean that he does not love the other parent. I believe that a skilled mental health professional is able to get a reliable response and should be able to uncover superficial motives. Is it really the red bicycle that is making the child say that he prefers one parent to another? A skilled professional goes beyond the words to the impressions that tell him what is going on in a child's mind.

"I've agreed to let my wife have custody of our children. We have worked things out so that my children and I will be together frequently. She and I have agreed that this will be best, since I love my children very much and they are close to me. However, my wife wants to move away to a city 1,200 miles from here. She feels she will have greater opportunities for building a new life there, but I am concerned that it will change the nature of my relationship with the children. Even if I could visit them frequently, 1,200 miles away, I would be seeing them in their home or in a hotel room rather than in my own home.

"I think this situation would be sufficiently damaging to my relationship with my children for me to refuse to accept the move as part of the divorce agreement. I know this will upset my wife, because she'll feel that I am trying to control her life by limiting the places in which she can live. How can this matter be dealt with rationally?"

If your decision to have liberal visitation arrangements was to preserve the integrity of your relationship with your children, it seems to me that any arrangements concerning the distance your children will be taken away to live should be based on the same consideration. Ideally, you should live close enough to exercise the visitation arrangements from your permanent home. Your children should be able to see you in your own home and should feel part of that home. Seeing you in a hotel room has a transient quality; your home provides a semblance of stability and is more reflective of you as a person and father.

Many concessions or compromises have to be made in divorce as well as in marriage. You and your wife would be acting in the best interests of your children if you both agreed not to move away beyond a certain distance from the city you are now living in, so as to provide continuity and stability for the children. If in the agreement you reach, both you and your wife are bound by the same restrictions, she will be less likely to feel controlled by you.

"Both my husband and I want our child, and I am willing to go to court to fight for him. But I am terribly concerned about what the litigation will do to our child psychologically."

That depends on whether your son is brought into the litigation procedure, and the grounds upon which each of you plans to seek custody. If either of you plans to prove that the other is unfit as a parent, then your son is put in a situation in which each parent demeans the character of the other. The litigation will involve the presentation of evidence by each parent about the incompetence of the other. No child can feel secure in such a situation. Even if attempts are made to keep your son from learning about the charges and countercharges, it is likely he will eventually learn what has been said.

On the other hand, if each of you is seeking custody on the basis of which parent is better suited to meet the needs of the child, the litigation will to a great extent involve evidence of a positive nature in support of each parent's competence. For obvious reasons, this kind of custody proceeding is less upsetting.

I don't believe a child should ever be brought into court to testify *against* either parent. Where charges of abuse to a child are submitted, every effort should be made to protect the child's right of privacy. Unfortunately, the legal machinery doesn't always lend itself to this kind of private testimony. Generally a witness brought before a court can be cross-examined by the attorney on both sides. In order for such testimony to enter the legal record, it must be given in the presence of both lawyers.

When a child is involved in the litigation, however, the court can apply a great deal of flexibility in the judicial procedure in order to protect the child. For example, the judge might allow the child to testify in closed chambers without the presence of either attorney and use that testimony in making his judgment. If matters are handled in this way, the child has an opportunity to express himself, and the decision will take his wishes into consideration. The judge must make it absolutely clear that the child is not deciding which parent he loves the most, but is providing information so that the judge can decide what are the best arrangements for his life after the divorce.

Some professionals feel that children should be kept out of litigation at all costs. I am not among them. While I believe every effort should be made to avoid it, there are many circumstances under which the child's participation is far better than the alternative—being left out of the procedure that will determine with whom, where, and how he will live. However, it is important for anyone who is planning custody litigation to remember that when the custody of a child is placed before a court, the parents relinquish the right to make any further decisions concerning the child and are, in a sense, at the mercy of the court.

"Now that it's too late, my husband and I, who are getting divorced, realize that neither of us is as child-oriented as we should be. Realistically, we shouldn't have had children in the first place. I think he is a far better parent than I am, and he thinks I am a better parent than he is. We are having a problem arranging custody because of this. We want to be fair to each other and also to our children. What's the best arrangement under these circumstances?"

As harsh as it may sound, I believe neither of you basically wants custody of your children. I find this attitude increasingly common. And for this reason I believe very strongly that we must teach young people about the responsibilities of child rearing during their formative years before they slip into parenthood.

The problem you are presenting is not a problem of divorce, but a problem of marriage. In all likelihood your children have recognized consciously or unconsciously your ambivalence about being parents. I would hope you have sufficient feelings of responsibility, whether they are based on guilt or not, to accept a plan that provides your children with the maximum feeling of acceptance.

While I don't think joint custody is the answer to everyone's problems, I think it may be the best arrangement under your circumstances. This need not be a permanent arrangement; during the period immediately following the divorce and for a few years afterward, various changes might take place requiring modification of this plan. If at the outset you each take equal responsibility for the care of your children, in all likelihood you will succeed in adjusting yourselves as the situation changes.

The most important consideration however is the feelings your children themselves have about where and with whom they would like to live. If each of you is able to maintain your emotional commitment to your children, they will ultimately be able to achieve a sense of independence that will be fulfilling to them and less demanding on you.

"I have custody of my seven-year-old son, and he has lived with me for more than one year now since our divorce. There has been no change in his behavior and he has not seemed at all worried, but all of a sudden the other day he said to me, 'I want to live with my Daddy—everything would be all right if I could live with my Daddy.' I don't know what to make of his remarks, and frankly I don't know how to handle the situation. What do you suggest?"

I certainly would not immediately pack his belongings and ship him off to his father, but at the same time I would not ignore his wishes or pass them off as a whim of the moment. Children sometimes try to manipulate parents or show hostility by expressing a wish to go to the other parent. While I believe it's important to take your child's statement seriously, you must evaluate it carefully. As objectively as you can and in an atmosphere of understanding, ask him to tell you more about his feelings. Tell him you will certainly consider his wishes seriously. However, let him know that you have to think the situation over, and that you might want him to talk to someone whose business it is to help children with their problems.

I suggest you consider having your son see a child psychologist or child psychiatrist to whom he can express his feelings more objectively than he can to you. In this way you can help determine whether or not his remark is simply a passing statement, or whether it represents a deep longing which is causing him underlying emotional distress.

If you act precipitously and immediately grant his wishes without evaluating the reasons behind his statements, he might get the feeling that it matters little to you whether he stays or goes. Only after a probing exploration of his true feelings will you be in a position to act responsibly and in his best interests.

Ideally the matter should be discussed with his father as well, but this of course depends upon the circumstances of your life and the nature of your relationship with your former husband and whether he wants custody. If you are on friendly terms, by all means bring this matter up. If it will precipitate a great deal of legal entanglement, it might be better to put off discussing it until you have evaluated the situation fully.

"My wife, who had custody of our two children, recently died in an accident. At the time of the divorce the children wanted to live with me, but I didn't want to go through a lengthy custody battle knowing I was unlikely to win. The children are now with me, but they feel I was forced to take them and don't really want them. They feel that if I had really wanted them, I would have fought for them in the first place. How can I get them to understand that I really want them even though I didn't fight to have custody of them?"

In some ways the situation you are faced with speaks well for parents who are willing to go to battle in their children's behalf. Perhaps to fight and lose in a custody matter is better than not to have fought at all. Many people avoid the struggle as you have, but for different reasons—to protect the *child* from the legal battle. As you can see, your children's feelings were more hurt by your compromise than if they had gone through litigation over custody.

I believe you have to let your children know honestly your reasons for not going to court in the first place. Assure them that you are very happy to have them now, although sad that their mother was killed. In time they will feel your love and acceptance and will understand the dilemma you were faced with at the time of the divorce.

From a psychological point of view, I believe your children's accusations are challenges to you to show your love and affirm your acceptance. They are caught in a psychological double-bind: they wanted to be with you in the first place, but their wishes only came true as a result of the death of their mother.

While they may be basically happy at the outcome, they probably feel guilty for feeling happiness that is tied in with the death of their mother. Looking at it from this viewpoint, you can see their dilemma and the need for the reaffirmation of your love and acceptance of them.

"After a great deal of hassling, compromising, and complicated bargaining, my husband and I worked out a schedule which gives him very liberal visitation rights with our children. What surprises me is that he rarely exercises these rights. I can't figure out why he made such a big fuss about it all and after telling the children how much he misses them, he doesn't show up or even call when he is expected. What does it mean, and how should I handle this?"

When a divorce takes place, each party tries to get the better settlement—to maintain as much freedom and have as many options open as possible. For this reason your husband probably struggled hard for the visitation rights he has. The fact that he doesn't exercise them suggests that his basic concern was to establish power over you, and not to remain close to his children. If he wanted to, he could see his children—the fact of the matter is, he doesn't, and therefore it is fair to conclude that other things are more important in his life than the visitation arrangements.

I am sure that it upsets the children when they have to wait around only to find that he doesn't show up. Moreover, it begs the question "Does my father care to see me in the first place?" If that question is put to you, I think it is fair for you to say, "I'm not really sure, but it would seem your father has other things which he prefers to do." While this may sound like a putdown of your children's father, I consider it an appropriate answer in the circumstances; it seems an inescapable conclusion.

It would only be confusing to your child if you were to make excuses such as, "I am sure your father would like to be with you, but something unexpected must have come up." How often can you make such a remark without having your children question your credibility? Your best approach involves being patient, supportive, but honest and frank in helping your children evaluate their father's behavior.

CHAPTER 7

DEALING WITH
THE LEGAL MACHINE

WHILE DIVORCE IS to a great extent a psychological process, by definition it is a legal process. It involves the dissolution of a marriage and all the products, commitments, and misunderstandings that were accumulated during its existence. People do not plan for their divorces at the time of marriage. For this reason, the specific details and plans for disassembling the marriage come all at once, and this can never be an easy process.

Everything you accumulated together needs to be divided. You now have to decide who gets what, and that can be as heart-rending as it can be nasty. Personal effects are easy to separate, but what about your wedding gifts and all those things given to you as a couple? Joint gifts from your children, including the things they made in school and brought home for you, are particularly hard to part with. Your books, your records, your photo albums; it is a very unpleasant task to go through each of these and decide whose it shall be. As things are pulled apart, you have a feeling that your part is now less than a fraction of the whole; what was a unity is becoming a shambles. Even if material things mean little to you, your belongings still carry an emotional link to the experiences associated with them.

As difficult as it is to resolve the division of property it is relatively easy in comparison with resolving the issue of your child's welfare following the divorce. Your property, your belongings, and other assets do not have feelings, although they may be viewed as the products of your marriage. You may have special feelings toward certain things, but basically it does not matter to your dining room table whether it goes to you or your spouse. That table has not established a relationship with you; you have established a relationship with it. Obviously the disposition of property does not have the human ramifications that divorce holds for your children.

When the decision to divorce has been made, the most important issue to face is the choice of a lawyer. I cannot tell you specifically how to go about finding the ideal lawyer. However, I would advise you to pick a man or woman with a great deal of experience in matrimonial law who seems flexible enough to consider the specific aspects of your case. You will not be well served by a lawyer who may simply slot your case into a category and deal with it in a very routine manner. You should also look for someone who has patience and will attempt to answer your questions and hear you out when your anxieties and fears build up. I know most lawyers prefer not to take on this "psychological" role, but they should give you a certain degree of

emotional support. In my experience, "hot-headed" lawyers serve no one's best interests; they simply agitate and
intensify feelings of animosity.

While some people might prefer to cooperate and nego-
tiate a divorce settlement, sometimes lawyers generate
more hostility than ever existed. Some lawyers are basically
"promoters" of conflict, and prey upon people who are
angry, desperate, or emotionally exhausted.

It is understandable that you'll initially want a lawyer who
is aggressive in your behalf, but probably everyone is better
off if the lawyers try to facilitate your goals, rather than
incite your adversary. It is all too common to find a lawyer
whose strategy is to wear down the other party with threats
and exorbitant demands. The showmanship among divorce lawyers is part of the ritual at times, and can deceive
you into believing you are better off than you actually are.
You can be incited into a frenzy, dragging matters out in
order to achieve those wild claims rather than reconciling
matters within reason. What might have been a mutually
agreeable divorce turns into an acrimonious battle of wills.

In the courtroom a person can feel emotionally vulnerable, very much at the mercy of the lawyers and judges. It
is with rueful regret that they recall seeking the counsel of
well-intentioned friends and relatives who urged "Take
him to court—you can't lose."

No lawyer can predict the outcome of litigation. A judge
bears the total responsibility of a decision once he has
heard both sides of the case. Be very wary of any lawyer
who tells you "You can't lose—you've got it in the bag," as
seductive as this may be. It's precisely the encouragement
you want to hear at a time when nothing is certain and you
are living in a state of suspended animation. Many matrimonial lawyers specialize in negotiating and will do anything to avoid going to court. However, some cases require

litigation for one reason or another, and it is therefore important for you to have an experienced litigator, if your case requires it.

One way of getting basic information concerning legal counsel is to approach your local or state bar association or the Academy of Matrimonial Lawyers to determine whom they consider specialists in this field. In law as in medicine, it is good to have a general practitioner to treat your everyday problems, but it is best to consult a specialist for a specific condition. You are bound to receive a great deal of advice from friends and relatives when it comes to picking a lawyer, which may or may not be helpful. I believe it is best for *you* to make the decision, based on your impressions after meeting with a few lawyers. You can always arrange a preliminary consultation, present your problem, and get some idea of the lawyer's approach, personality, and most important, your reactions to him or her. I do not think it is necessary to find a lawyer who "warms your heart," but I do believe you should have a lawyer in whom you have a good deal of trust.

I have emphasized the issue of choosing an appropriate lawyer because I feel that lawyers play a very significant role in divorce proceedings. I respect people who assert themselves and try to solve their problems using their own resources, and the "do it yourself" divorce is becoming increasingly popular. It is seen as an alternative to the high cost of legal fees. Another common concern is that a lawyer will not represent a client's best interests as well as the client himself can. From what I have observed, the men and women who act as their own lawyers get hopelessly entangled in court procedures and probably encounter more problems than if they acquired responsible legal counsel.

As a matter of principle, I do not recommend the "do it yourself" approach. It's not exactly the same as trying to remove your own appendix, but it can be just as ill-advised. I believe the old expression "A person who acts as his own lawyer has a fool for a client." Get yourself a lawyer who is experienced, who is a specialist in marital matters, and whom you feel confident in.

For the most part, the laws governing matrimonial matters are, to say the least, antique. They were devised over a long period of time and have been highly resistant to change. I do not mean to be critical of the legal and judicial professions. It takes a great deal of time and money to go to court to challenge existing laws in order for change to take place. Few people are willing or able to take on such a burden. Unfortunately, after years of handling divorce cases many lawyers and judges only look at the superficial elements of a case and draw conclusions from them. They become desensitized to the extenuating circumstances and complicated human issues which are at the very heart of divorce but which are not easily taken into consideration.

Our society needs to develop a greater congruence between its laws and the changing mores and life styles. We are living in a fast-moving society, but our laws lag behind. The discrepancy between the two creates an area of potential injustice that can cause undue suffering for everyone involved in matrimonial matters, particularly children.

For example, mothers have traditionally been the ones who spent the most time with the children. The mother has always been the primary caretaker of the children, and it is generally assumed that she will continue to devote the same time and effort to them after a divorce. This is an incorrect assumption. When the structure of the family changes, the roles of the family members also change. The mother may very well get a job after her divorce and engage in many outside activities which require paid overseers for her children. In fact, this situation often occurs after a divorce. The mother not only is no longer spending the majority of her time with her children, she may in fact be spending less time than the father would if he had custody of the children. Assuming that the father works away from home, he too would be absent for many hours of the day and have to hire paid help to care for the children.

I raise this latter point simply to demonstrate the inflexibility of traditional thinking in evaluating the circumstances of family life after a divorce. Judges and lawyers who engage in matrimonial work frequently fail to take into consideration the most salient issues that affect the well-being of the children. They apply hard-and-fast rules in the disposition of custody matters, but their judgments may well be based upon an outdated norm rather than on the individual needs of the given case.

Other legislative fields seem more able to adjust and update their methods to deal with changing problems. There are frequent changes in tax laws as well as major efforts at tax reform to meet the needs of our society. In fact, tax lawyers and accountants are hard-pressed to keep abreast of the modifications in the law. It seems to me that in the area of matrimonial law similar efforts at reform are sorely needed.

Our legal system has been totally inadequate in recognizing and meeting the needs of children. We have specialists in medicine and dentistry to deal with children's problems —pediatricians and pediodontists—and perhaps we should have a specialist in law, who could be called a "pediattorney." The advantages of such a specialty would be mandatory psychologically oriented training and experience about children leading to certification or a license. We would then have skilled professionals who realize that children's needs are different from those of adults and who know how to deal with these needs. A child may have a hard time articulating his feelings about how he wants his life to be organized after a divorce. In order to express his feelings honestly and directly, he needs the guarantee of privacy to assure himself that the court-appointed professionals are sincerely interested in working things out to his advantage. If such a procedure were to become part of the normal course of a divorce case, custody matters could be more easily resolved in favor of the child.

Whoever interviews the child should make it clear from the outset that everything discussed between them will be confidential and that his parents will not be told. A child would normally fear that whatever he says would get back to his parents and might cause one or the other to reject him.

In my professional experience I have often been consulted by lawyers and parents on custody matters and been asked to make recommendations concerning the welfare of the children involved. I always talk to the child in the privacy of my office and immediately make it clear that what we discuss will not be discussed with his parents. I assure him that I will recommend what I consider to be the best arrangement—the one that will make him happiest. When I am placed in this position, I must have the support of the parents in protecting the child's right of privacy. As difficult as it may be for the parents to accept, I cannot stress enough how important it is for the child's future happiness.

Judges also need special training. Ideally, it should be the judge who makes the decision concerning custody. I would hope that in the future judges will be required to receive training similar to that which I suggested for lawyers in order to handle this responsibility adequately. This is not impractical; it can be accomplished through seminars, workshops, and training sessions to provide skills in developing interview methods for children, together with the necessary knowledge required to evaluate their emotional needs. Such training should be mandatory for anyone dealing with family law. In addition, courts dealing with matrimonial matters should have skilled professionals available to offer additional assistance in assessing the needs and wishes of children.

While progress has been slow in the evolution of legal procedures consistent with our changing society, there has been progress in this direction elsewhere in the world. In some countries there is no need to prove who is to blame for the dissolution of a marriage; all that is needed is a sworn statement that has been in effect for one year declaring that neither party intends to continue the marriage. The major advantage to this approach is that the children are more likely to be protected from possible dissension. A counseling service is also available to the parents to help them work out the child custody issue. Consequently few people go to court over a divorce, and are therefore spared the substantial court costs and legal fees common in this country. Under this system, children are not automatically given to the mothers; in fact, in approximately half the cases they are awarded to the fathers. The deciding factors are the life style of each parent, their financial resources, and the closeness of the relationship between the parent and the child. In addition, children's wishes concerning the parent they want to live with are respected.

I am convinced that sensitive people, trained to use the tools for greater human understanding, would be effective adjuncts in our courts in making judgments and assisting people in the reorganization of their lives. Children whose parents end up in divorce court would be happier, more successful individuals if our legal system were tempered with humanity in the course of exercising justice.

Dealing with the legal machinery in divorce is very stressful for many people. In my professional consultations, I've been presented with numerous problems on the subject, some of which are discussed below.

"My lawyer wants me to bring an action against my husband to remove him from the house while we are trying to get the divorce. He wants me to change the locks on the doors, and claim that my husband is dangerous and violent. My husband does not really act that way, but my lawyer says it would look better for me for the final settlement if I do this. He says it's done all the time. I know it would upset my children and infuriate my husband. I am in a mess and don't know what to do."

When a divorce becomes acrimonious, the adversaries frequently jockey for position. What your lawyer is suggesting is not uncommon. Fortunately, however, courts don't always grant such a motion unless substantial evidence is given. In your case, you would have no evidence, and it sounds to me as though you are not emotionally disposed to do it in the first place. The fact that it would upset your children and infuriate your husband tells me that it's an unwise move. Eventually your children would resent you for your action, and in no way would it make them closer to you. By infuriating your husband you would be pushing him further away from you, making communication more difficult.

Whether you won such an action or not is less important than the fact that it would create greater upset for your children. Assume for the moment that you won the action, even though you know that your husband is not a violent person; your deception would be paid for in the long run. If you were to bring the action but lose it, you would have declared war on your husband, provoked him to respond, and then lost the first battle.

When taking such an action against another person, you have to give consideration to the long- as well as the short-range effects. In this case everyone would lose, your children in particular.

"I've heard so many people complain about their lawyers and I don't know what to do about the legal mess of my divorce. My wife moved to another state and took the children with her. The lawyers I've talked to seem vague about how it's all going to turn out. I'm inclined to handle the whole matter myself and forget about lawyers. I think I can learn enough by reading a few books and talking to some people who have been through it themselves. I think I'd be in better control of the whole matter, and I'd save a lot of money as well. What would you advise?"

You need legal counsel. The legalities surrounding a divorce are generally very complicated, filled with technicalities, burdened with time-consuming details often involving long delays and periodic postponements—all of which is sufficiently confusing that you cannot go it alone. The backlog of cases alone is large enough to cause certain delays and cursory dispositions of important issues.

To complicate things further, legal systems vary from state to state. I would strongly advise that you hire a lawyer to protect your interests and those of your children, especially in your circumstances, where the children have been moved without your consent.

"My wife and I can't come to any agreement about some of the personal problems affecting our lives and our children's lives. In principle, I consider it wrong for someone like a judge to decide for us how to handle such personal problems. A judge could not possibly understand the complete history behind our problems or the relationships we have with each other. Why should he be placed in a position of making such important decisions about our futures?"

I understand your point completely, and partly agree with you. I sympathize with your concern that some stranger with his own history, values, and prejudices will be placed in the position of determining the fate of you and your children. This is, in fact, what happens when matters concerning a divorce and custody of children are placed before a court. In effect your children become wards of the court, and each parent is expected to abide by whatever decision the court makes. For this reason many people try to avoid bringing a custody matter into court and will do everything within their power to work out the arrangements either by themselves or with the assistance of lawyers and other professionals.

While there are drawbacks to court jurisdiction over a child's life, there are also certain advantages, particularly when parents are in sharp disagreement on matters concerning their children. The court is then in a position to represent the child's interests. We can only hope that legal procedures will evolve so that greater care will be taken to assess all the elements in the life of each family member.

"I've recently heard the story of three children who were living with their mother after a long and bitter court fight. The father decided to hire a professional 'child snatcher' to go to the playground and have his children picked up bodily, put in a car, and driven across the state line to where he lived. There was little the mother could do under the circumstances other than have the children 'snatched' back. How disruptive is this procedure of child snatching to a child?"

Very disturbing. It is extremely traumatic for a child to be picked up by a stranger—in effect a kidnapper—and taken away from his home. He could suffer crippling anxiety following this traumatic experience, every moment of his life filled with the fear that he is about to be snatched again. Child snatching is cruel, and there should be strict penalties for it.

Fortunately, legislation is moving in the right direction. Many states have passed laws recognizing a custody decision made in another state, so that a parent gains nothing by moving a child to a different state to start a custody proceeding there. Unfortunately, there are still some situations where one parent can have custody in one state while the other has it in a different state, and neither state honors the decision made elsewhere. If custody decisions in a given state were honored in every state, children would be protected from this kind of legal Ping-Pong and we might see a sharp reduction in child snatching.

"I am a lawyer specializing in matrimonial matters. I frequently run into clients who seem to revel in the miseries of divorce, and I'm convinced they manipulate their lives so that nothing ever works out. I find it difficult to counsel these people and would like to know your thoughts about people like this and what your experience has been."

This is perhaps the most difficult client to deal with—I call him the "injustice collector." This person has built his life around various "injustices." He takes the normal, everyday injustices all people face and constructs a whole life style around them. There seems nothing one can do that he cannot transform into an injustice. And if he's involved in a divorce, his spouse of course is the greatest offender; since he feeds on contrived grievances, every step of the way becomes a delicious opportunity to reinforce his self-righteousness. Apart from the discomfort this can cause, it is almost impossible to keep injustice collectors from weaving their own children into their collection of injustices.

One parent who consulted me about her difficulties in dealing with her children through her divorce presented a picture of her husband as an absolute villain. When I tried to get her to give me the specific details of what she meant, she became very evasive. I pressed harder and harder, and finally got a response. I asked her to give me an example of what she meant by his having to control *everything.* She said, "Throughout our marriage he did a lot of the cooking, and he always cooked things he liked—he never cooked anything he didn't like!" I asked her whether she enjoyed his cooking. She admitted that for the most part she did, but re-emphasized the point that "he never cooked anything he didn't like!" This was to her unjust.

I decided to pursue my quest for facts and not interpretations. She had said, "He gives me *nothing* for food for myself and the children." When I finally cornered her with "You mean absolutely not one cent?" she admitted that he gave her something, but she wouldn't consider it anything. As it turned out, the sum he gave her solely for food far exceeded what a family of five would require for an average week. When I pointed this out to her, indicating that it should be sufficient for three people, she said, "But I consider that *nothing.* "

This type of person sometimes revels in divorce. It is an opportunity to gain sympathy, and injustice collectors are usually effective spokesmen for their side. Few people probe to get the actual facts and are easily misled by the injustice collector's interpretation. These lurers of sympathy tend to remain fixated in the morass of their divorces and have a hard time moving into a life style that provides them with an opportunity for positive growth and development. In fact, in most instances the divorce resulted from their lack of growth within the marriage itself.

Certain people have difficulty appreciating what they have in a relationship with another person. Their preoccupation is with all the things that are wrong with the other person and all the things they do not have. While it may be difficult and at times impossible to deal with such people, at least one can recognize injustice collectors and begin to understand the dynamics of such personalities.

"I know my husband is a liar and he is running around our town telling everyone his side of our problems. What do I do to counteract the lies he is telling? Our court case is now scheduled and I feel powerless to get anyone to believe what really happened. What do I do?"

Generally speaking, a person who acts in this manner was a chronic liar long before his present troubles. He is not only capable of believing his own lies but he is very adept in telling lies and generally comes across very credibly. Needless to say, this is a difficult situation for you, since it presents a terrible barrier in dealing rationally with the problems you face, particularly those concerning your children. You feel great anguish and frustration when faced with lies that you know are absurd. It places you in the position of being very defensive, and sometimes a defensive attitude can lead people to suspect that perhaps *you* are not telling the truth.

It is not uncommon for some lawyers to encourage their clients to be florid in describing their marital difficulties before the judge. This is particularly true when court proceeding involves judging one person's word against the other. Friends, too, may prod one party to exaggerate and even lie about events that took place in the marriage in an attempt to gain strength over the adversary.

"There are two sides to every story," and the truth generally lies somewhere in between; so states the conventional wisdom. In counseling many parents through divorce I have learned that, on the contrary, there are *not* always two fair sides to every story. One parent may be meticulous about the truth, while the other is a blatant liar.

While there is little you can do about your husband's lies at the present time, you can take heart in the fact that liars tend to destroy themselves. Very often under cross-examination during a trial a liar will get confused over his story and will be exposed for what he is. I can only tell you that a liar will eventually lose his credibility.

"I am a lawyer whose main practice is handling matrimonial matters. After years of experience I feel confident in my knowledge of technical legal information but I still feel inadequate counseling my clients when it comes to the delicate matter of their children. Looking at my profession from your viewpoint as a psychologist, how can I learn to deal with the issues concerning children more effectively?"

The hardships that children experience in divorce result to a large extent from the fact that lawyers, judges, and other legal professionals have little or no knowledge of the emotional nature of children. Moreover, they are not skilled in interviewing or observing children, and can be even somewhat intimidated by them. It is far easier for judges and lawyers to place children in the category of property and deal with them accordingly.

If we are truly concerned about the effect of divorce on children and truly want to minimize the negative effects, legal training will have to include the study of human behavioral development, with emphasis on the changing needs of the growing child. The custody and welfare of the child after divorce should be handled as a separate issue from alimony and other divorce-related issues. A mental health professional should be the one to evaluate the total situation and assist in determining custody.

CHAPTER 8

PREPARING FOR YOUR LIFE AFTER DIVORCE

YOUR LIFE STYLE AS a married person developed gradually. In a sense, you had the opportunity to plan for the development of your home, your work life, your social adjustment, and the advent of children. Obviously, some people handle these matters more systematically than others, but everyone has some sense of control over the situation and can generally avoid being overwhelmed by too many responsibilities at any given time. Immediately following a divorce, this situation changes abruptly.

That which you built gradually seems to come apart all at once. Your new life style as a single person begins to take on a quality you did not expect. After living in a marriage that was unfulfilling, conflict-ridden, or stifling, it is easy to anticipate that divorce will bring great freedom, boundless joys, new opportunities for self-expression. Most of all, you look forward to the tremendous relief from the stresses and conflicts that you experienced before. Your fantasy of liberation is not totally a fantasy, but it takes time to get there. In all likelihood, you do experience a sensation of freedom, but this is quickly supplanted by new and different concerns. Whether you are male or female, or whether you have custody of your children or not, your life style has just changed and you must be prepared for a period of disorganization.

The key to making the best adjustment in the shortest period of time is to prepare yourself realistically for the problems and responsibilities you will encounter following divorce. Those problems cover a broad range: there will be the practical problems of your everyday life and the personal problems involving your emotional readjustment and the developing of a new and different social life.

Perhaps the most important change after divorce takes place in the relationship between you and your children. Much of the change is a result of your new living arrangements and the amount of time you spend together. As a single parent you have a greater burden of responsibility for their emotional as well as their physical welfare.

While the practical problems vary from individual to individual, all single parents are faced with the task of providing shelter, food, clothing, and care for their family without the help or involvement of another person. These tasks can be a substantial drain on your time and can certainly cause emotional stress, particularly if your previous life experiences provided inadequate preparation. All of a sudden you find there are bills to be paid, laundry to be washed, repairs to be made, none of which were previously your responsibility; these tasks take up an increasingly large amount of time, possibly having an adverse effect on your performance of your job, or keeping you from outside employment altogether.

I am a strong supporter of educating our youth in mandatory school programs in matters concerning food, clothing, shelter, and care of the young. I call such a program "human survival training." While such training is useful under any circumstances in life, I believe it's of particular value in the event of divorce. It would provide males and females with a greater knowledge of how to function responsibly as the sole provider in a family, which in turn would substantially minimize many of the stresses that people encounter immediately following divorce.

As a divorced parent you may feel that your parental role multiplies into what seems to be many roles. This is not the case. What *has* changed considerably is the amount of responsibility—for some it's less, for others more. While the single parent who has custody of the child may have greater continuity in his or her life before the divorce, that parent is placed in the position of having to assume a much greater responsibility; responsibility not only for the physical well-being of the child, but also for his emotional needs. If in the aftermath of the divorce the presence of the child contributes to the parent's feelings of depression, guilt, resentment, and loneliness, that parent must nevertheless attend to the needs of the child.

Obviously, if the parent who has custody of the child sincerely wanted custody and the child preferred being with that parent, this difficult situation will be more easily resolved. On the other hand, if the custodial parent has ambivalent feelings about the child or subconsciously would have preferred the other parent to have custody, it is far more difficult for that parent to deal with the child's emotional needs. The same is true if the custodial parent is not the preferred parent as far as the child's feelings are concerned.

The parent who does not have custody, but who sees the children periodically, clearly has greater freedom to establish a new life. Superficially, this may seem simpler and more gratifying, but many people in this situation are faced with loneliness and a deep sense of loss of the family atmosphere. Some parents report such an intense fear of being alone that they are driven to seek out almost anyone who can supply even momentary companionship. They are plagued with doubts that anyone cares about them and wonder "What would happen if I got sick, would anyone help me?" The fears of abandonment and loss of love are not unlike those of a child in a divorce situation. Parents look forward to the stabilizing effect of visits with their children. One father claimed, "Even if I see my children one day a week, it's so good to hold on to that little element of family life." Children are sensitive to these parental feelings and frequently take on the task of offering comfort and compassion to the parent.

Over and over again parents living alone state that conquering loneliness is the single greatest challenge following divorce. As difficult as the loneliness is, it's even harder to control feelings of anger and jealousy when your child tells you about the wonderful times he's having with his other parent's new friends. It is perhaps the most difficult of all to accept another person's taking over your parental position as the new partner of your ex-spouse.

The parent who does not have custody also can feel threatened that his children will move far away, making visitation exceedingly difficult if not impossible. The major emotional problem in divorce for a parent is the possible loss of the children as a result of the separation. Losing the spouse through divorce may be a blessing, particularly after prolonged marital tension, but the absence of the children can cause severe emotional upset.

While not as important as your relationship to your child,

your personal and social life is also in a state of transition. The friends you and your spouse had during your married life frequently drift away from you because your life style has changed. You no longer have the same interests. As a single person, you may have trouble adjusting to being alone at parties and gatherings, and if you include your "dates" in social events with these friends you may find a prevailing awkwardness. Your dates were not part of your past friendships and can feel left out; there could be some subtle resentment expressed by these dates, since they are essentially replacements for your ex-spouse. You may also find your friends passing judgment on your dates, which increases the pressure on you. Your social needs are different now. You may have a wish to meet more people, and may find that the pattern of your previous social life doesn't lend itself to your new interests.

In general, divorced people find it easier to socialize with other divorced people because there is greater understanding of the responsibilities and problems involved in this new life style. The divorced parent with custody of a child can be somewhat of an enigma to a person who does not understand the emotional commitment to the child. While it might be more enjoyable for the parent to go to a movie or a party, his or her child may need help with her homework that night or need some additional time and attention to talk about the normal concerns children have. I am not advocating self-sacrifice and total involvement with the children at the expense of all other involvements for the custodial parent. This would place a tremendous burden on a child; no child wants to feel that he is the sole source of all your pleasures or miseries. By the same token, if you focus solely on your own changing needs and life style you may cause your child to feel left out or rejected.

Many parents are afraid to begin dating because they fear

their children will resent sharing their parent with someone else. I know of one case in which a ten-year-old girl refused to go to sleep when she found out her father had begun dating again and she might no longer be "Daddy's girl." Although the father was not the custodial parent, the daughter felt sufficiently threatened to disrupt her own life. Some parents are worried that if they establish too many relationships, or do not sustain them for any length of time, they will confuse their children. In all likelihood, your children will be happier if you are happier. The parent who has good communication with a child is able to discuss the new relationships and emphasize the fact that although friends may come and go, parents are permanent.

Your children will be more flexible than you think in accepting your new friends into their lives, and you may be surprised to find that they encourage you to have more friends as your social life brightens. If you are depressed, lonely, or generally unhappy, your children may feel that it is their responsibility to bring joy into your life. Since they can't fulfill all your social needs, your persistent unhappiness can lead them to feel guilty—as if they have failed in making you happy. Ideally they would like to see you happy with other people, so long as it does not *cause them to feel left out.* For this reason, as your life style changes and you begin to socialize more, do what you can to incorporate your children, as appropriately as possible, into your social life.

In recent times we have developed a greater understanding about the needs of all human beings for close relationships and sexual satisfaction; it's important for children to feel that these desires are normal and natural and should not in any way arouse shame or embarrassment. Many parents are confused about how to deal with their sexual needs after a divorce, particularly when it comes to having friends stay overnight or join the family on vacations and trips. At such times it's rarely possible to keep a child from knowing that the parent is sleeping with someone. Parents often avoid any sexual contact or emotional involvement, rather than risk upsetting their children. Yet children are generally more accepting of a parent's close physical relationship with a companion than they anticipate. This is particularly true if the child feels secure, receives a great deal of affection, and doesn't feel the companion is someone he must compete with for attention and love.

If you have your child's trust and respect, there need not be any problem for your child in accepting your sexual needs. If you have answered your child's questions concerning sex and reproduction in an atmosphere of acceptance and understanding, he or she will have no difficulty knowing that a special friend on occasion may spend the night with you at home. The same applies on trips and vacations. Obviously, a steady turnover of people who flow through your bedroom can phrase a different message from that associated with deeper emotional relationships and special friendships.

Children react positively to those circumstances which serve as an emotional enrichment of their own lives. Clearly, this is a positive existence, and probably a far cry from the atmosphere that existed during their life with you before the divorce. Parents who incorporate children into their friendships and make their home environment more lively generally find that the children do not cling to them as much or react negatively to the times the parent chooses to go out alone with a friend. You should encourage your children to socialize with their friends as well and to bring them into your home. Most children enjoy having a home that is filled with happiness. Being able to share this atmosphere with their friends not only enhances their self-esteem but serves to encourage more peer interaction.

To some, all this may sound as if your whole life must revolve around your children in order for them to make an adequate adjustment to divorce. That is not true. I do believe, however, that a substantial part of your life with your children requires a sharing of responsibilities and pleasures—whether you are married or divorced. I believe *very strongly* that during the transition period and immediately after the divorce you have to make a concentrated effort to establish in the minds and hearts of your children that you not only care for them, but are capable of giving them the love, acceptance, and attention they need.

Once it is clear to your children that they *belong* and that you are available to meet their needs, they will be increasingly tolerant of your expanded interests outside the home, and in many ways they will appreciate the independence and freedom it gives them to do things on their own. You remain close to your children by meeting their needs, yet allowing them to move away from you, as their growing need for independence emerges.

As your life style changes, you should take care not to relax your responsibilities toward your children. If you are the custodial parent it is important to uphold the same rules and regulations you had before, maintaining the same discipline as well as the same expectations of your child. A parent who feels guilty or is fearful of rejection by his or her children will tend to overindulge them; the children are confused as a result and more vulnerable to uncertainty.

If you are not the custodial parent you may feel the need to program every moment of your child's visit with activities, resembling a three-ring circus. It is common for parents who sorely miss their children to use visits to assure themselves of the children's continued affection for them. The temptation to buy them anything they want, take them anyplace they care to go, and indulge them with anything they want to eat is indeed great. However, it's important to avoid this kind of overindulgence: it serves the parent's need more than the child's. One experienced divorced father claims it's best to do things *with* the children rather than *for* them; his children especially enjoy playing games with him and having him read to them. He deliberately resists buying a lot of things for them so they will not view him solely as a provider of material things.

In dealing with the other parent through the divorce and the period of adjustment later on, avoid competing for the child's affections and favor. Some parents try to outdo each other and win their children over to them by indulging them—for example, offering them foods and treats which many children like but which were previously forbidden because they are unhealthy. I have seen such behavior backfire more often than not. The child demands material things when he needs love because you've taught him that these two needs are interchangeable. Rarely, if ever, does a child feel you love him as a result of material indulgences. Furthermore, overindulging your child puts him in a position where he can manipulate one parent against the other, expressing favor for the one who gives him the most.

Overindulgent behavior is disquieting to children. They clearly sense your anguish and despair, and your desperation comes through with the flurry of forced activities or your showering them with gifts. What they really want and need is being *with* you. Sharing experiences and talking together mean so much to a child.

It is best if both parents respect the child and share with him rather than compete over him. Even if only one parent acts wisely and is able to take a hard-and-fast line to support the integrity of the child, success can be achieved.

I cannot prescribe the ideal life style for anyone, nor can I elaborate on what you should, or should not, do as a divorced parent. However, it's important to remember that divorce in many instances is a positive solution for a family crisis, and as painful as it may be at first, the restabilization of family life offers the child a far greater opportunity for happiness than could ever be achieved by maintaining a conflict-ridden marriage.

In re-establishing your life after divorce, remember to bring your children into your life as much as possible. Let them feel close to the work you do, the responsibilities you have, and the friendships you develop. Show a concerned interest in their lives, including their friends, school, and other interests, but do not stifle them in the process.

Children need to develop the sense that they belong to you, and that you are a loving, protective parent who is there when they need you but who is able to let go little by little as they develop security and a desire to function more and more as an individual.

If your new life is fulfilling and you share it with your child, his sense of belonging serves as a pattern for his own life. He will know what happiness is, and have a more optimistic outlook on family life than if he were burdened by living in a miserably unhappy family, grimly determined to remain together for the sake of the children. A child's feeling of belonging to two parents, even though they may live apart, is the best possible outcome of the divorce.

The period of adjustment after divorce is very difficult for many people. Some of the problems presented by patients in my professional consultations are included in the following questions and responses.

"I understand that a very high percentage of divorced people when they remarry make the same mistakes in their new marriage and have a high divorce rate for their second marriages. This worries me because I am divorced and plan to remarry, but don't want to become another divorce statistic. How can I best avoid this?"

These statistics are somewhat hard to interpret and can be very misleading. Obviously, people who don't get divorced don't remarry and logically can't get divorced a second time. Moreover, at least some of the group who have never divorced may be tied by religious or social convictions, social pressures, or economic factors that preclude divorce.

It is a fact that many people tend to repeat the same mistakes they made in their earlier marriage, without understanding how some of their underlying emotional problems contributed to the difficulties. For this reason, many people go for counseling or psychotherapy after their divorce in an attempt to gain insight into their own role in the marriage that failed.

In my opinion people who rush immediately from a divorce into remarriage without having known the new partner for any length of time are more prone to make mistakes. Other people are so hesitant to enter into a relationship after a divorce that I suspect that too may be a sign of some repressed emotional problem. I believe it's very wise to get professional help if you have any doubts or questions about repeating the same pattern.

"I am concerned about how you help a child adjust to having multiple parents after divorce. My ex-wife has remarried and so have I. Each of the people we married has other children near in age to our own. We keep running into problems because my new wife sets different rules and regulations to run our household than my children were used to. My ex-wife complains that she has the same problem. In addition, when my new wife insists that my children carry out certain household responsibilities they usually reply, 'Who are you to tell us what to do? You are not even our mother!'

"Frankly, the children seem to be getting away with murder because we don't know how to handle their disobedience. At times I am not sure whether they enjoy the situation and the control they have over us, or whether they are anxious and unhappy because of inconsistency in handling them. Is this situation insurmountable?"

No, not entirely. But it is important to recognize that you have a difficult situation on your hands. To begin with, I am sure that you want your new wife's children to accept you and are inclined to avoid confrontations over discipline. Some people in the role of new parents tend to overindulge their "new" children in an effort to be liked and accepted. It's as difficult for the parents as it is for the children. Everyone involved wants to be accepted but is also testing the new family members and looking for injustices and inconsistencies.

I feel that the best way to avoid confusion is to continue to use the old rules and discipline as a base for your new family structure. Consequently, the children will be inclined to enjoy the indulgences and protest at the more stringent limitations that the new parents offer. You can be sure that both sets of children will make comparisons between their new and old families in an effort to exact greater leniency. For example, expect such comments as "You are a meany, Mom. When I am at Dad's house, his new wife doesn't force me to go to bed at any special time—why should I have to go to bed at nine o'clock here?" The best approach to this problem and all others arising out of the readjustment to new family members and multiple families is not to feel intimidated, angry, or defensive but to stand by the rules that you find appropriate to your life style.

If you accept the children and show respect for their feelings, in all likelihood they will adjust to your standards and appreciate the consistency in your treatment of them. Make it clear that whatever happens in the other house with their other parent has nothing to do with what you set up as standards of acceptable behavior in your home. When faced with the remark "You are not my mother—so why should I do what you tell me to do?" don't hesitate to say, "Yes, I know I am not your mother—I am your father's new wife, and no one will ever replace your mother to you. But that doesn't mean I can't tell you what to do in my house." You might point out that teachers are not the pupil's parents, but they too set limits on what is acceptable behavior, and that there are many other situations and circumstances in life where acceptable behavior is not defined only by parents.

At times you may feel that the children are baiting you. As malicious as you feel it to be, understand that it's an attempt on their part to test you and find out what your strengths are. If you lose your temper, become overly punitive, or in some way show a loss of control, you will have allowed them to get the better of you. Try to ride with their complaints, discuss matters as much as you can, but don't hesitate to stand firm on the things you believe in.

As difficult as it is, with patience and understanding you can eventually establish a comfortable living arrangement with your new family. Realistically speaking, however, there are some children who never seem to be able to accept a new parent, and some parents find that they can never really warm up to a new child. Professional psychological help is extremely worthwhile when these apparent incompatibilities persist.

Time plays an important role in the working out of these problems. Don't expect a positive adjustment immediately. In fact, if you are surprised by a smooth transition, brace yourself for the fact that it won't last and that you will have to go through some period of turmoil in order for everyone to work out all their feelings and come to terms with these new relationships.

"The economic changes we've undergone as a result of our divorce have caused us to alter our life style substantially. I never realized to what degree we would be affected by this, since few of my friends who have divorced have mentioned this particular problem. We have had to give up our summer place, can no longer take holiday trips during the children's Christmas and Easter vacation, and have even had to move into smaller quarters, where the children have less privacy. Will this have any substantial negative effects on my children?"

Not necessarily. In general, children are more interested in the activities they engage in than the expense behind them. I suggest you allow your children to participate in the planning of new kinds of activities that you can comfortably afford in your new circumstances. If they take on a responsible role in the planning of these activities, they will be quick to accept the changes. Don't harp on the fact that things aren't as easy as they were, but focus instead on the brighter side of things, and the whole process of change can become pleasantly adventurous. For the most part, children enjoy camping in the woods more than they do spending an equivalent time in a luxury hotel. Most communities offer social, athletic, and cultural events that cost little or nothing. From a child's point of view these can be just as enjoyable, if not more so, as expensive seats in a famous concert hall.

Having to share a room with a sibling when the child used to have his own room is probably one of the hardest problems. It too can work out to everyone's advantage if you make it clear that there are simply no alternatives but that you are open to their suggestions. From time to time there will be the inevitable problems when children have to share close quarters, but that is to be expected.

"My children have seen me weeping over the breakup of our marriage. They reassure me that they love me and that they will help me become happy again. Isn't this too much of a burden for them to worry about me, when it should be the other way around?"

I don't think that it is at all bad for your children to be sensitive to your unhappiness and try to reassure you. Their reassurance may reflect a desire on their part for similar reassurance from you. I know that many people, including professionals, would consider this a big burden to a child, but I personally feel the weakening of family unity is in part due to the fact that family members seem to feel that it's "mature" to be unconcerned about one another's feelings.

If a child feels important within a family unit and indeed finds that he can help ease the discomfort or anguish of a parent, or any other family member for that matter, it strengthens his bond with him or her. In recent decades we have moved away from that kind of family unity. It's to be hoped we will move closer to re-establishing family ties, sharing in the pleasure and pain, joy and anguish, of the people we are closest to.

"My thirteen-year-old daughter and I have lived together alone since my husband and I were divorced three years ago. For the most part we have gotten along well, but no matter how hard I try, I just can't get her to participate in any activity with me as a family unit. After all, she and I *are* our family and I want desperately to give her the feeling that we are such a unit. When I ask her advice on buying new curtains, she simply shrugs her shoulders and says she doesn't care. She is not interested in joining me when I have a dinner party for some of my friends. She simply goes off to her room and avoids me as much as she can. What can I do to get her to share more with me than food and lodging?"

To begin with, it's important for you to determine whether she is in fact avoiding you or whether she is simply showing the temporary solitary behavior typical of some teenagers. Or perhaps her behavior reflects resentment toward you for splitting the family up and placing her in a position of greater responsibility as your sole family companion.

I think you should discuss your feelings with her and possibly seek outside help to devise a way that both of you can become happier living together. While she may respond that she is happy the way things are, you can still impress upon her *your* wish to get help and that you would like her to join you. In evaluating the situation, keep in mind that your daughter may well be reacting normally and that perhaps you are over-reacting in your desire for greater companionship during this period.

There is no solution to this situation until you get greater insight into her reactions and your own feelings about it. While many children do behave this way, there are also a multitude of emotional problems that could be covered up by "I don't care."

"It seems to me that life is one change after the other. No sooner do you adjust to one situation than you're faced with something new. Isn't there some theory or knowledge that will help us understand ourselves better in disruptive situations like divorce?"

There are many transitions from the familiar to the unfamiliar which take place in the natural course of events; beginning with birth itself, you are propelled from the protected, nourishing womb into a world filled with different sounds, smells, and tastes where your life will never again be so protected or secure.

Going to school for the first time, graduating from school, marriage, parenthood, and retirement are some of the transitions that occur in life. These are all stressful situations.

Some time ago, I conducted studies with colleagues to determine what happened to a person at retirement; we found that the way a person dealt with a transition at retirement correlated to his ability to handle all the previous transitions he had undergone in the course of his life. The people who were able to make the transitions smoothly were realistic about themselves, in terms of both their weaknesses and strengths; the ones who experienced transitions fraught with psychological and physical symptoms of stress were, in general, those who had an unrealistic concept of their abilities, their strengths, and their weaknesses, and tended to focus on events in their past or project themselves far into the future, rather than using the present as their point of reference.

Perhaps the most enlightening part of our study was the insight we gained into the period of turmoil that follows a transition. We found that a period of turmoil was normal if one was to realistically accept and efficiently adjust to the change brought about by the transition. Initially we had expected the most effective transitions would be those with the least amount of turmoil; this was not the case. The group who did not experience turmoil around the time of transition were unable to accept the actual transition—in fact, these people reacted as if the transition did not take place. In effect they denied what had happened, and eventually they were faced with a state of psychological shock that remained with them over a long period of time. They tended to live in the past and made a poor adjustment as compared with the group that experienced turmoil at the time of transition.

While the situation of divorce is not precisely analogous to retirement, some of the knowledge we acquired about understanding the psychology behind periods of transition is applicable to divorce.

INDEX